THE POE TWISTED ANTHOLOGY

EDITED BY
ENRICA JANG

CONTENT WARNING

REDSTYLO
m e d i a

Published by Red Stylo Media
Cold Spring, NY

© 2011 Red Stylo Media
ISBN: 978-0-9829564-1-0

Editor:
Enrica Jang

Cover Art:
Andrew Jerz, Alex Cormack, Phillip Jacobson, Enrique 'Zeke' Savory Jr.

Cover and Book Design:
Enrica Jang

Printed in San Francisco CA by KENESS, www.Keness.com

twistedpoe.com
redstylomedia.com

DEDICATED TO POE FOLK EVERYWHERE:
ALL THOSE WHO LOVE THE DARK MASTER AS MUCH AS WE DO.

CONTENTS

iNTRODUCTiON

DON'T CALL IT ADAPTATION.

Adaptations are a retelling. Perhaps in updated, new ways, but adaptations are, at their heart, the same story told again. **POE TWISTED** is something different. A challenge to a new crop of writers and artists to be inspired by Poe rather than simply retell him.

"Take the characters or setting from your favorite Edgar Allan Poe story, twist them, and make something new." Sounds easy, but you have to have a healthy ego to take on the original, undisputed master of American gothic and crime fiction. Poe's work is canon.

Hubris is a beautiful thing. Rather than taken over by him, **POE TWISTED** takes turns with him. Everyone who has read and loved an Edgar Allan Poe story or poem has come away with an image that haunts, a turn of phrase that excites or stings. Our Poe-tributors take their favorites and imagine new ways to twist the stories or characters, discovering more. The result is this collection of horror and hilarity, touched by the dark genius of the master, and yet with many an ironic jab and poke at him too. A parody here, a sequel there, but all of the pieces mutated re-imaginings of Poe characters in new worlds. Or Poe worlds in new characters.

And why comics? Poe is an immortal genius who lives on in the brooding, dark images he created with words alone. We pay tribute, we aspire, but in the end we paint the pictures for you (six times in this collection with actual paint.) There's only one Edgar Allan Poe.

continued next page

This anthology is not a primer for new Poe readers. We're not updating him, or introducing him to a new generation. POE TWISTED stands on its own as a collection of graphic stories and vignettes, dedicated to lovers of Poe's work and for all the different things Poe as literary figure has come to represent: the macabre, the disturbing, the crime-licious, the insane.

If we've done our job, you'll finish this book with a burning desire to go back and read your favorite Poe tale again. And if you're a fellow Poe Folk artist or writer and think you can do us better…bring it on.

Here's my address:

EDITOR@TWISTEDPOE.COM

Yours in Poe,

ENRICA JANG

"TAKE THY BEAK FROM OUT MY HEART, AND TAKE THY FORM
FROM OFF MY DOOR!"

QUOTH THE RAVEN, "NEVERMORE."

from "THE RAVEN"

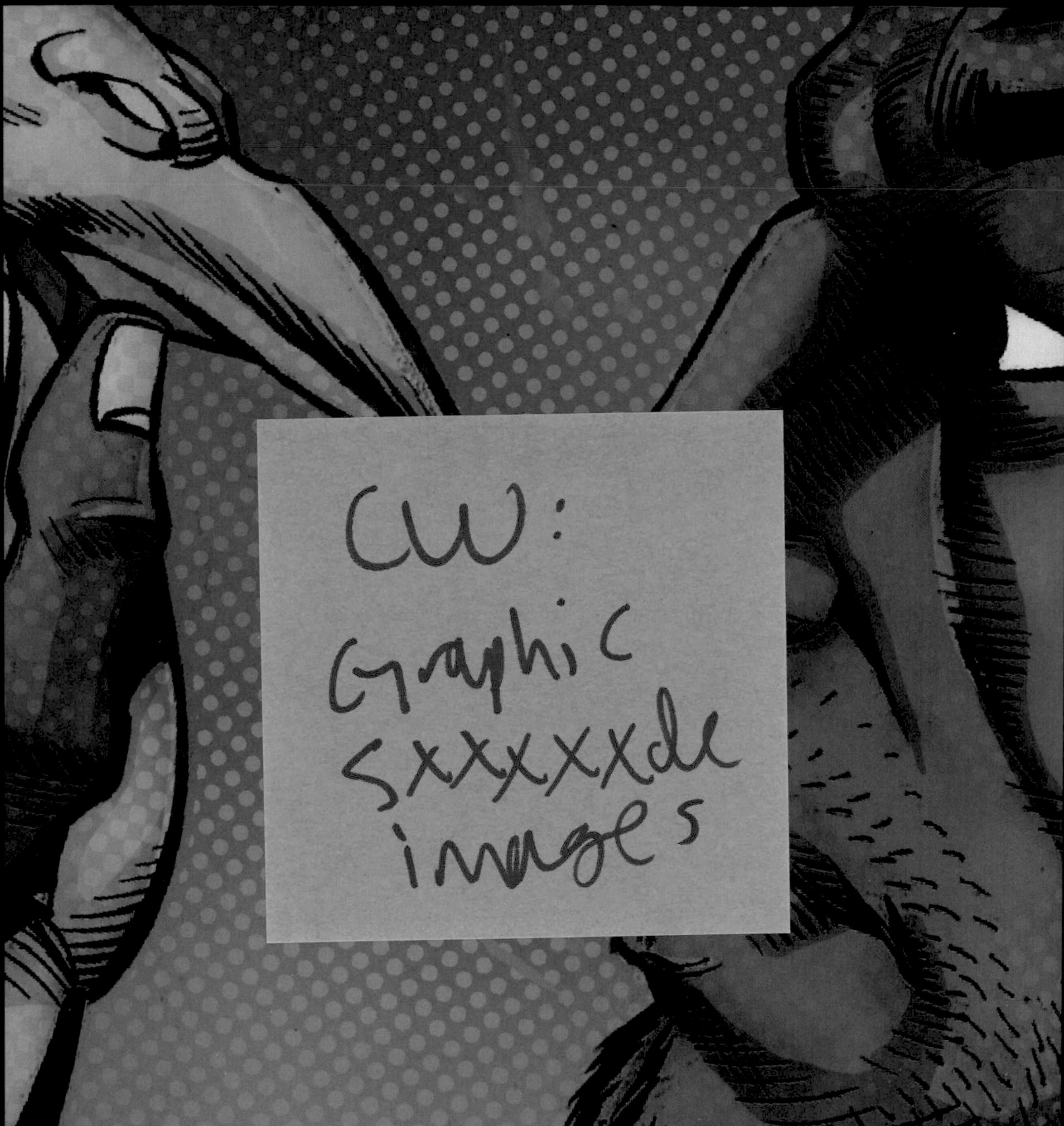
CW:
Graphic
Sxxxxxde
images

ABSOLUTION

JASON CIARAMELLA ENRIQUE 'ZEKE' SAVORY, JR.

ALEX CORMACK ANDRE FRATTINO

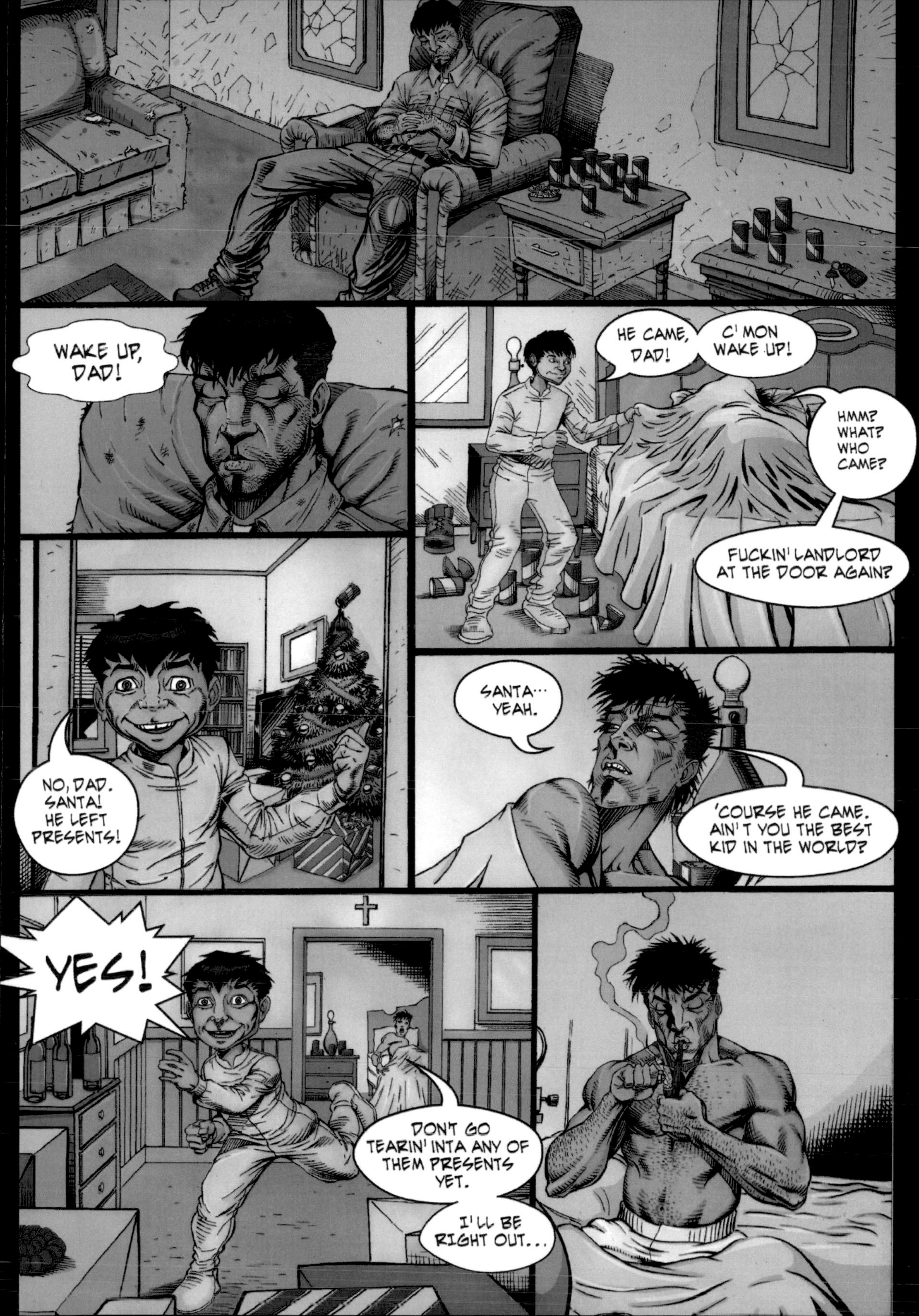
WAKE UP, DAD!
HE CAME, DAD!
C' MON WAKE UP!
HMM? WHAT? WHO CAME?
FUCKIN' LANDLORD AT THE DOOR AGAIN?
NO, DAD. SANTA! HE LEFT PRESENTS!
SANTA... YEAH.
'COURSE HE CAME. AIN'T YOU THE BEST KID IN THE WORLD?
YES!
DON'T GO TEARIN' INTA ANY OF THEM PRESENTS YET.
I'LL BE RIGHT OUT...

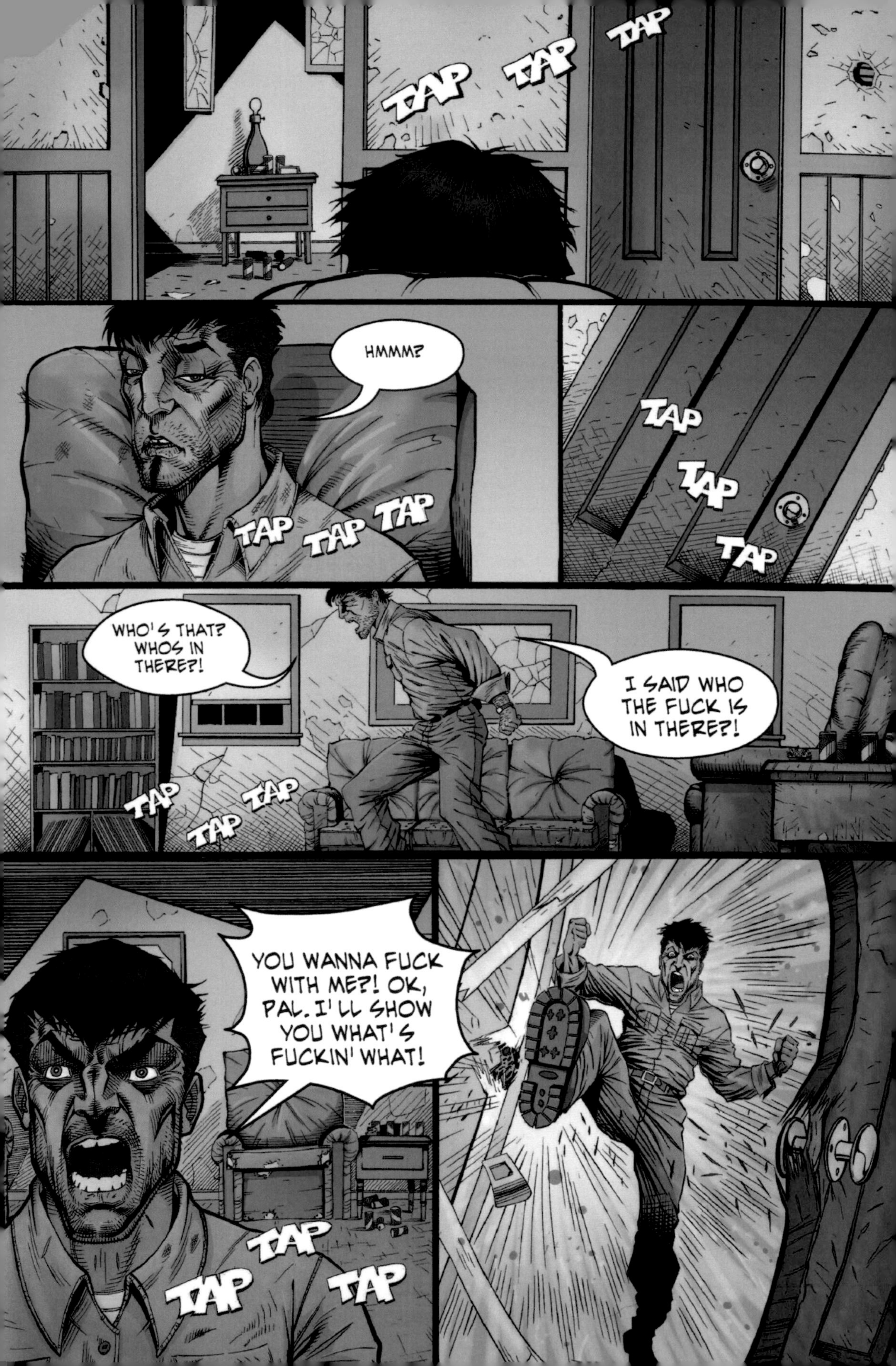
TAP
TAP
TAP
HMMM?
TAP
TAP
TAP
TAP
TAP
TAP
WHO'S THAT? WHOS IN THERE?!
I SAID WHO THE FUCK IS IN THERE?!
TAP
TAP
TAP
YOU WANNA FUCK WITH ME?! OK, PAL. I'LL SHOW YOU WHAT'S FUCKIN' WHAT!
TAP
TAP
TAP

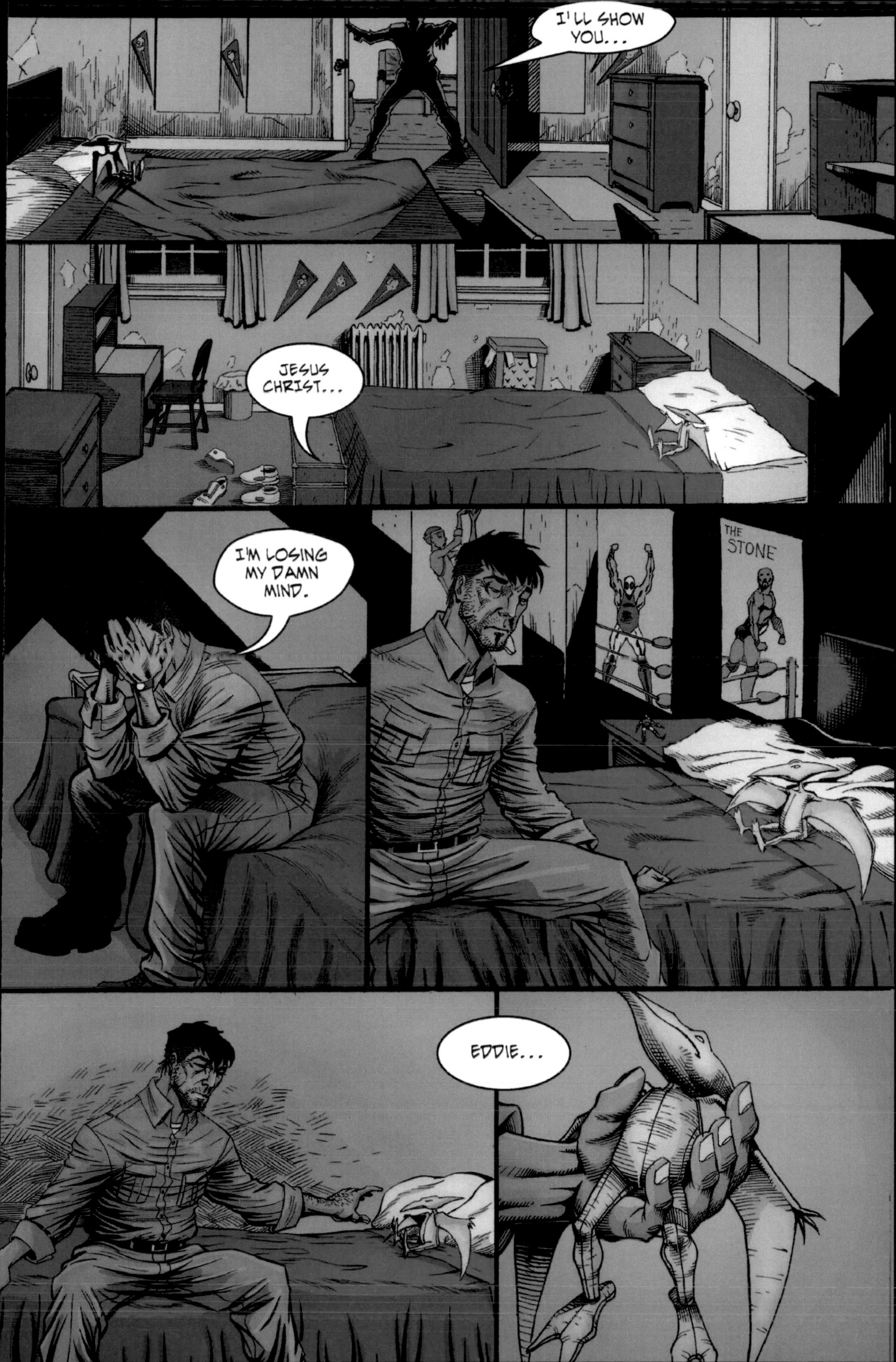
I'LL SHOW YOU...
JESUS CHRIST...
I'M LOSING MY DAMN MIND.
THE STONE
EDDIE...

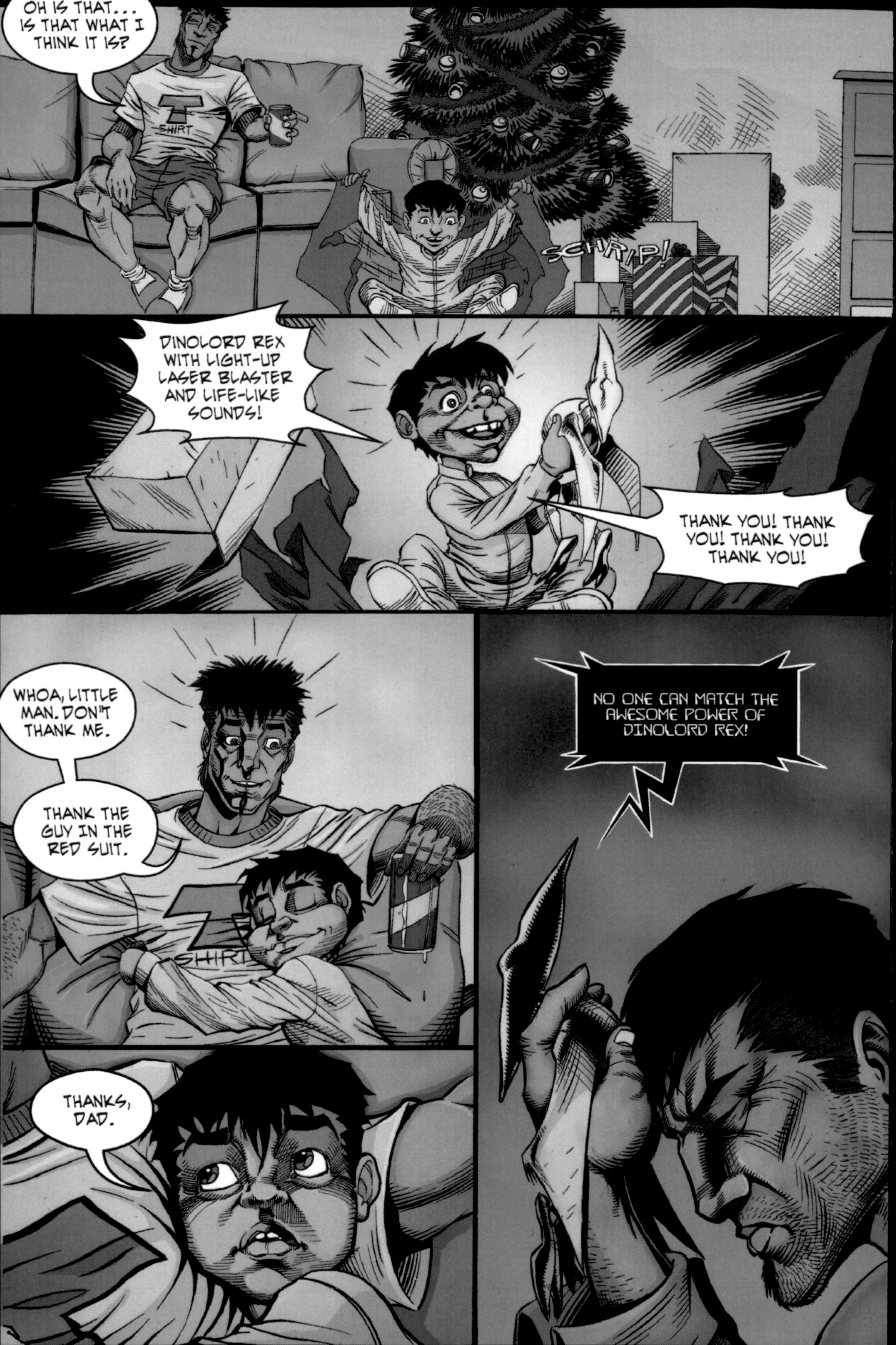
OH IS THAT... IS THAT WHAT I THINK IT IS?
SCHRIP!
DINOLORD REX WITH LIGHT-UP LASER BLASTER AND LIFE-LIKE SOUNDS!
THANK YOU! THANK YOU! THANK YOU! THANK YOU!
WHOA, LITTLE MAN. DON'T THANK ME.
THANK THE GUY IN THE RED SUIT.
T SHIRT
NO ONE CAN MATCH THE AWESOME POWER OF DINOLORD REX!
THANKS, DAD.

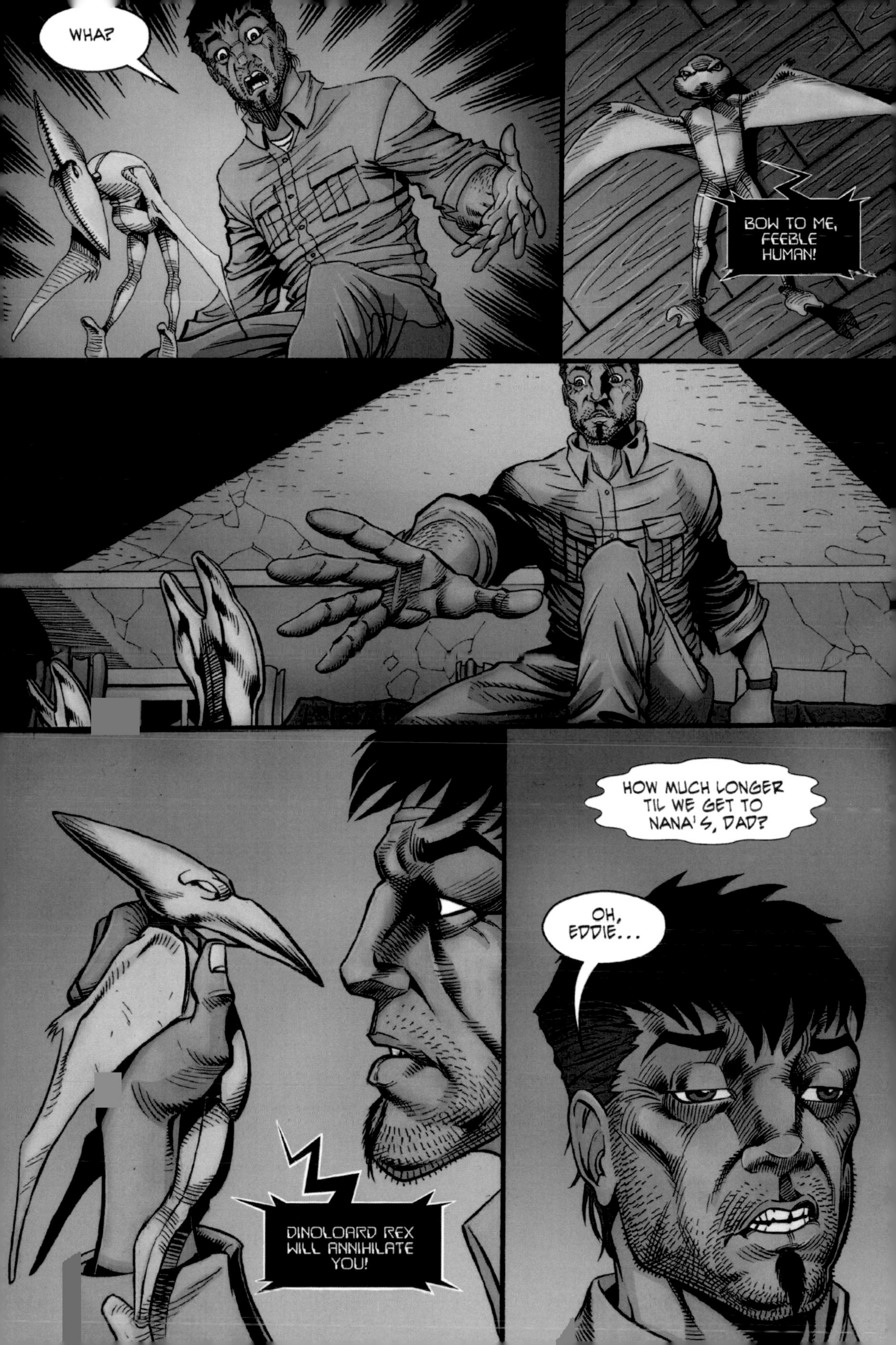
WHA?
BOW TO ME, FEEBLE HUMAN!
DINOLOARD REX WILL ANNIHILATE YOU!
HOW MUCH LONGER TIL WE GET TO NANA'S, DAD?
OH, EDDIE...

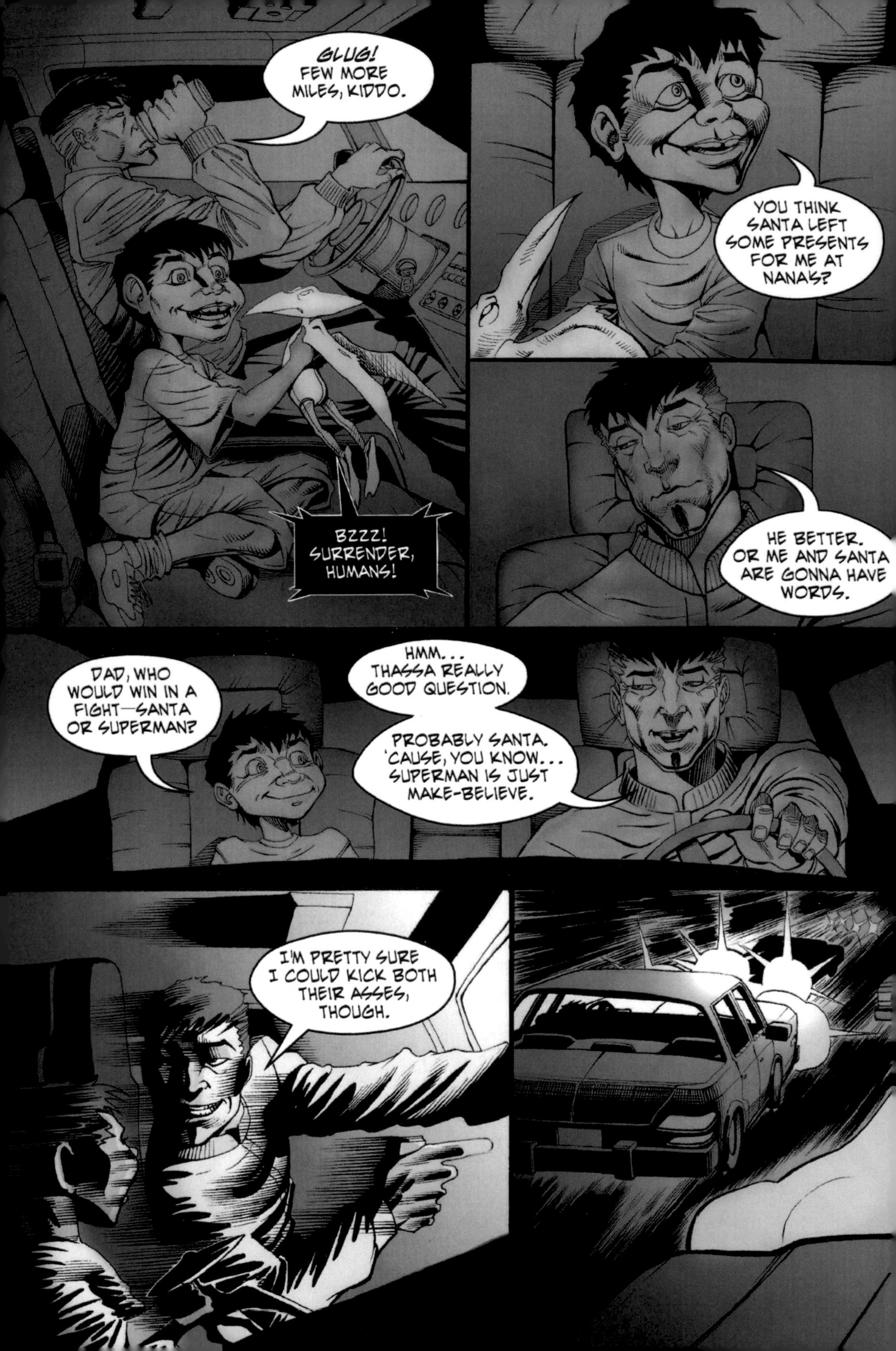
GLUG!
FEW MORE MILES, KIDDO.
BZZZ! SURRENDER, HUMANS!
YOU THINK SANTA LEFT SOME PRESENTS FOR ME AT NANA'S?
HE BETTER. OR ME AND SANTA ARE GONNA HAVE WORDS.
DAD, WHO WOULD WIN IN A FIGHT—SANTA OR SUPERMAN?
HMM... THASSA REALLY GOOD QUESTION.
PROBABLY SANTA. 'CAUSE, YOU KNOW... SUPERMAN IS JUST MAKE-BELIEVE.
I'M PRETTY SURE I COULD KICK BOTH THEIR ASSES, THOUGH.

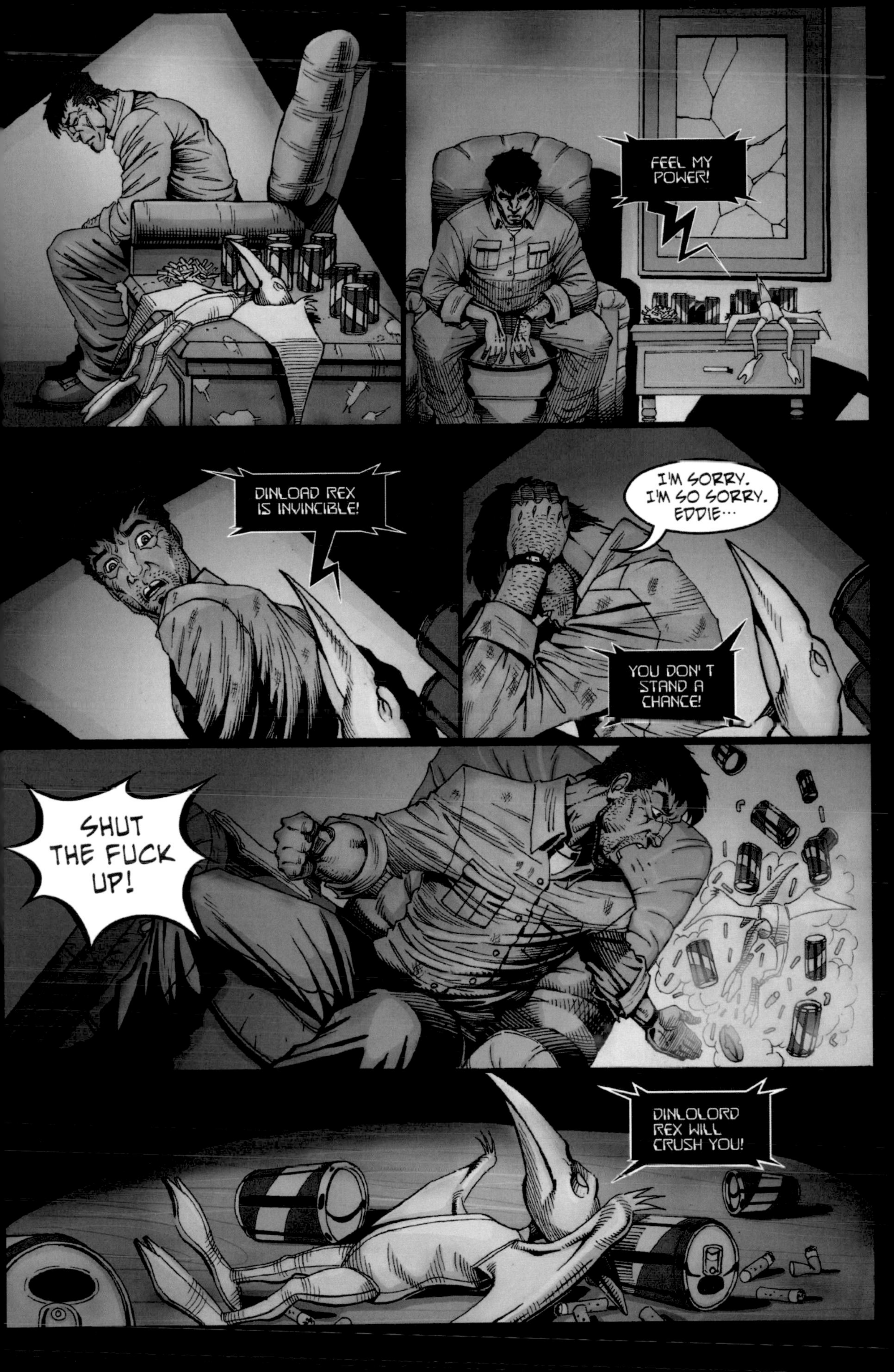
FEEL MY POWER!
DINLOAD REX IS INVINCIBLE!
I'M SORRY. I'M SO SORRY. EDDIE...
YOU DON' T STAND A CHANCE!
SHUT THE FUCK UP!
DINLOLORD REX WILL CRUSH YOU!

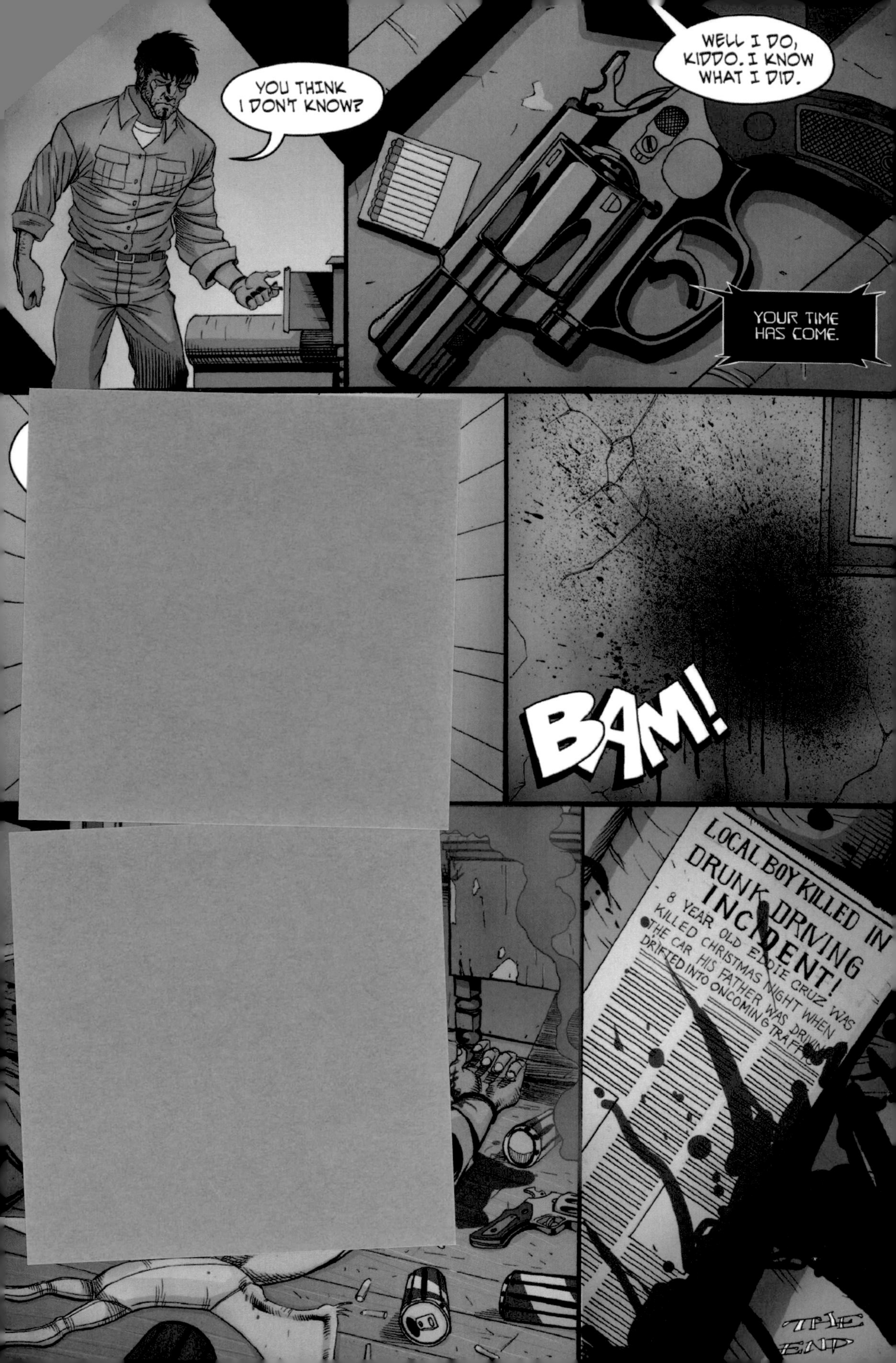
YOU THINK I DON'T KNOW?
WELL I DO, KIDDO. I KNOW WHAT I DID.
YOUR TIME HAS COME.
BAM!
LOCAL BOY KILLED IN
DRUNK DRIVING INCIDENT!
8 YEAR OLD EDDIE CRUZ WAS KILLED CHRISTMAS NIGHT WHEN THE CAR HIS FATHER WAS DRIVIN
DRIFTED INTO ONCOMING TRAFF
THE END

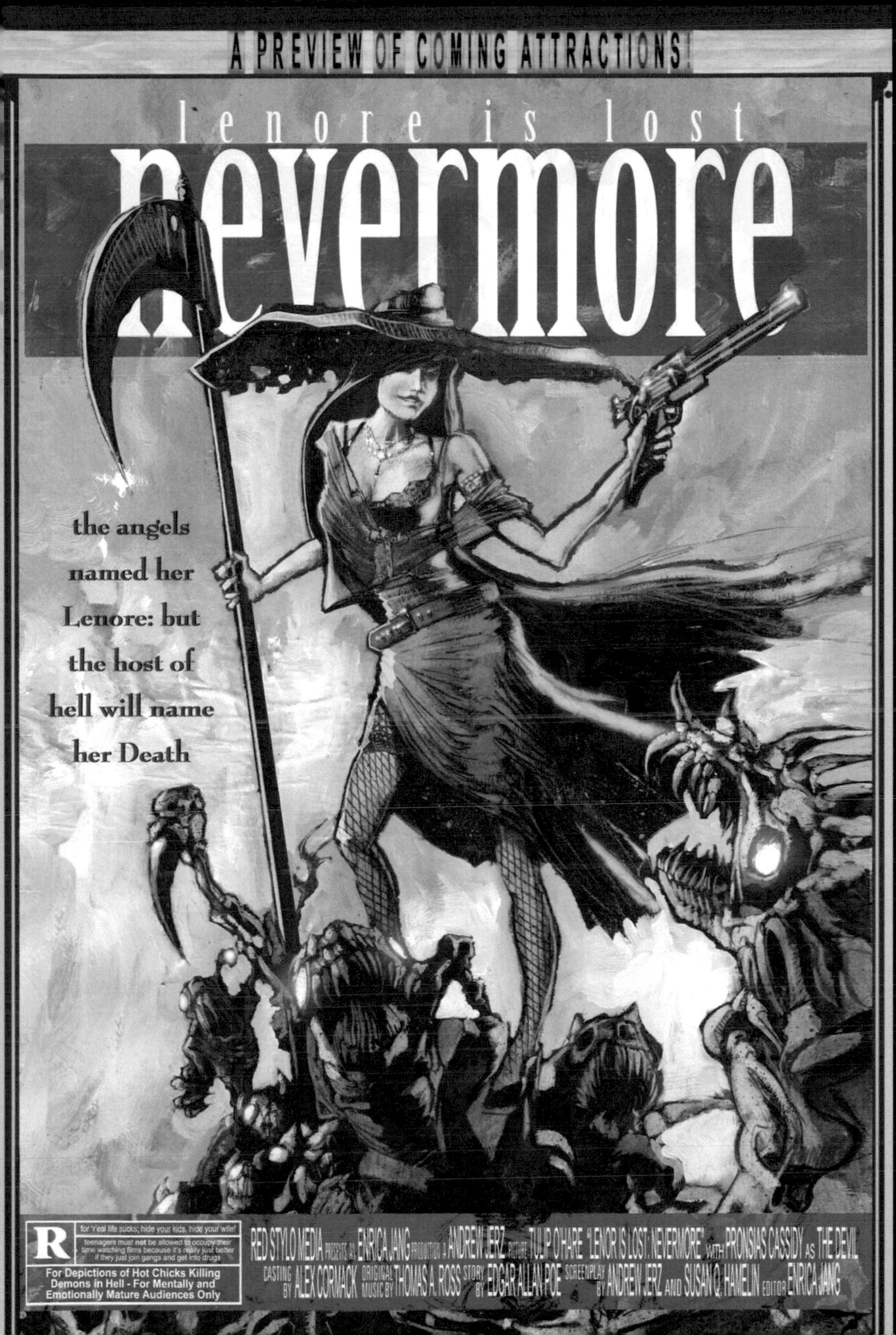
A PREVIEW OF COMING ATTRACTIONS!
lenore is lost
nevermore
the angels named her Lenore: but the host of hell will name her Death
R
for 'r'eal life sucks; hide your kids, hide your wife!
teenagers must not be allowed to occupy their time watching films because it's really just better if they just join gangs and get into drugs
For Depictions of Hot Chicks Killing Demons in Hell - For Mentally and Emotionally Mature Audiences Only
RED STYLO MEDIA PRESENTS AN ENRICA JANG PRODUCTION A ANDREW JERZ PICTURE TULIP O'HARE "LENOR IS LOST: NEVERMORE" WITH PRONSIAS CASSIDY AS THE DEVIL
CASTING BY ALEX CORMACK ORIGINAL MUSIC BY THOMAS A. ROSS STORY BY EDGAR ALLAN POE SCREENPLAY BY ANDREW JERZ AND SUSAN Q. HAMELIN EDITOR ENRICA JANG

HAD ANY ONE TAKEN HIM UP, HIS HEAD WAS SMALL, AND THUS HIS LOSS WOULD HAVE BEEN SMALL TOO.

from "NEVER BET THE DEVIL YOUR HEAD"

DEAD MAN'S HAND

STORY AND ARTWORK BY PHILLIP JACOBSON

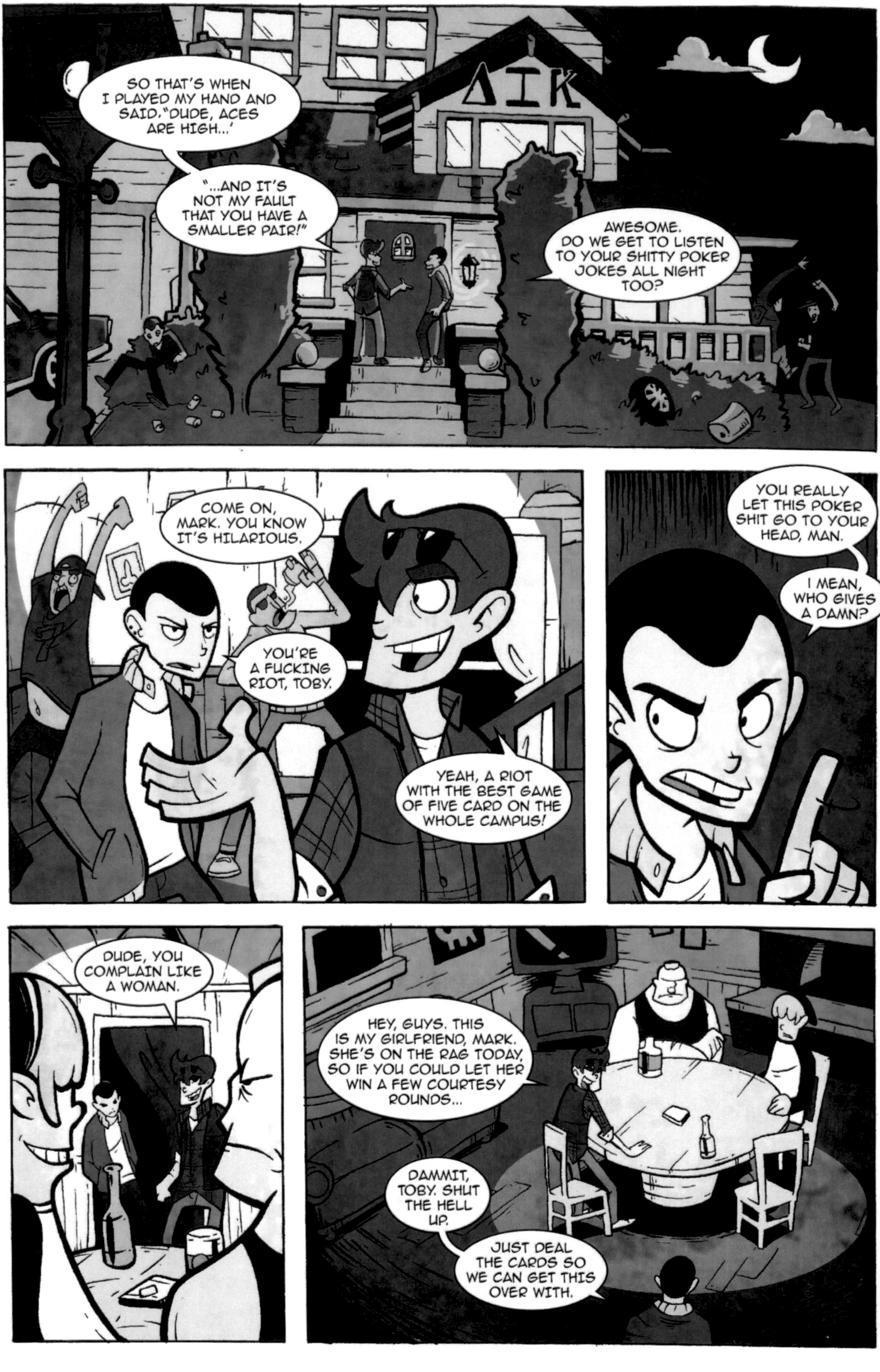

SO THAT'S WHEN I PLAYED MY HAND AND SAID, "DUDE, ACES ARE HIGH...'
"...AND IT'S NOT MY FAULT THAT YOU HAVE A SMALLER PAIR!"
AWESOME. DO WE GET TO LISTEN TO YOUR SHITTY POKER JOKES ALL NIGHT TOO?
COME ON, MARK. YOU KNOW IT'S HILARIOUS.
YOU'RE A FUCKING RIOT, TOBY.
YEAH, A RIOT WITH THE BEST GAME OF FIVE CARD ON THE WHOLE CAMPUS!
YOU REALLY LET THIS POKER SHIT GO TO YOUR HEAD, MAN.
I MEAN, WHO GIVES A DAMN?
DUDE, YOU COMPLAIN LIKE A WOMAN.
HEY, GUYS. THIS IS MY GIRLFRIEND, MARK. SHE'S ON THE RAG TODAY, SO IF YOU COULD LET HER WIN A FEW COURTESY ROUNDS...
DAMMIT, TOBY. SHUT THE HELL UP.
JUST DEAL THE CARDS SO WE CAN GET THIS OVER WITH.

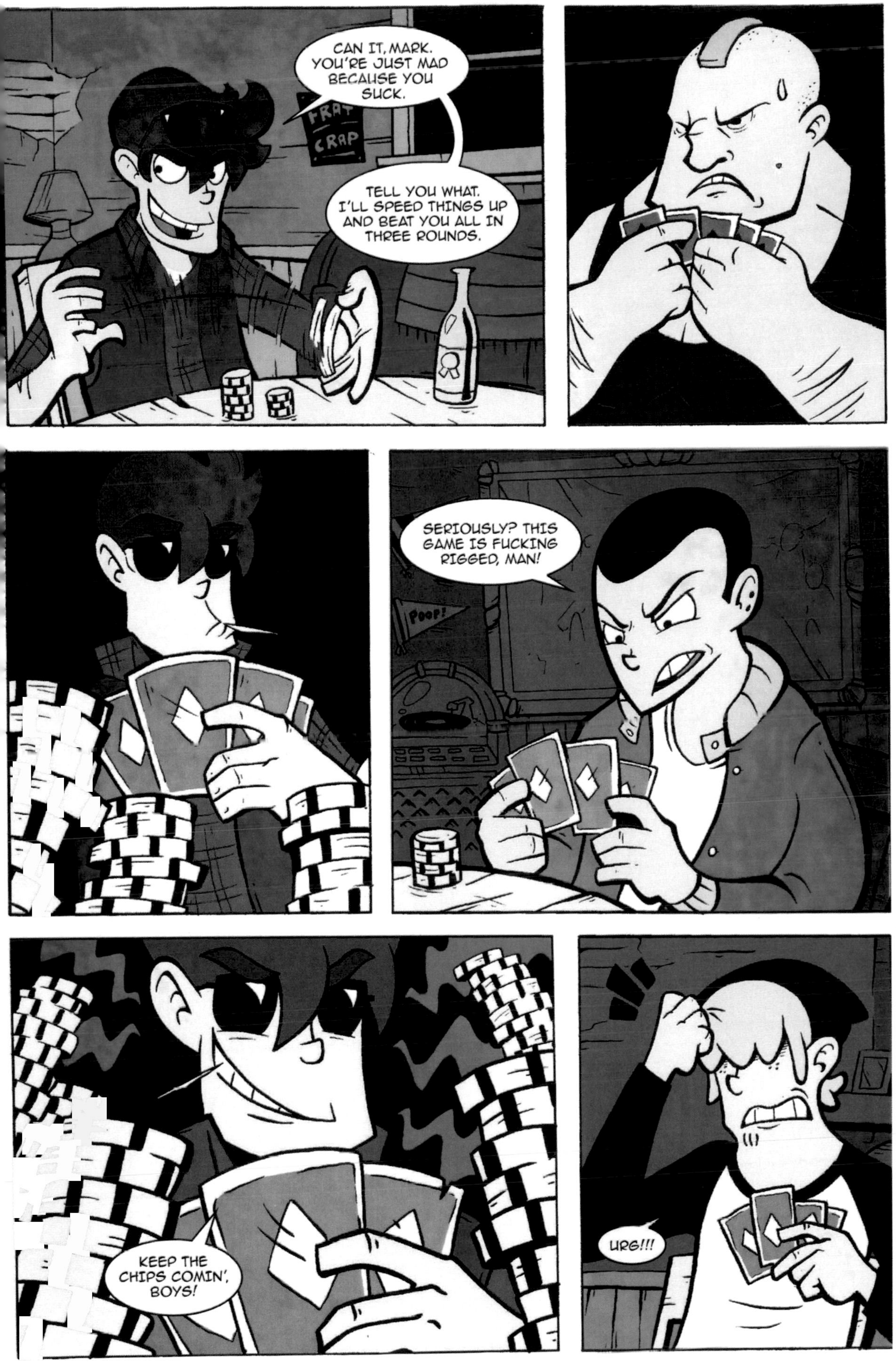
CAN IT, MARK. YOU'RE JUST MAD BECAUSE YOU SUCK.
FRAT CRAP
TELL YOU WHAT. I'LL SPEED THINGS UP AND BEAT YOU ALL IN THREE ROUNDS.
SERIOUSLY? THIS GAME IS FUCKING RIGGED, MAN!
POOP!
KEEP THE CHIPS COMIN', BOYS!
URG!!!

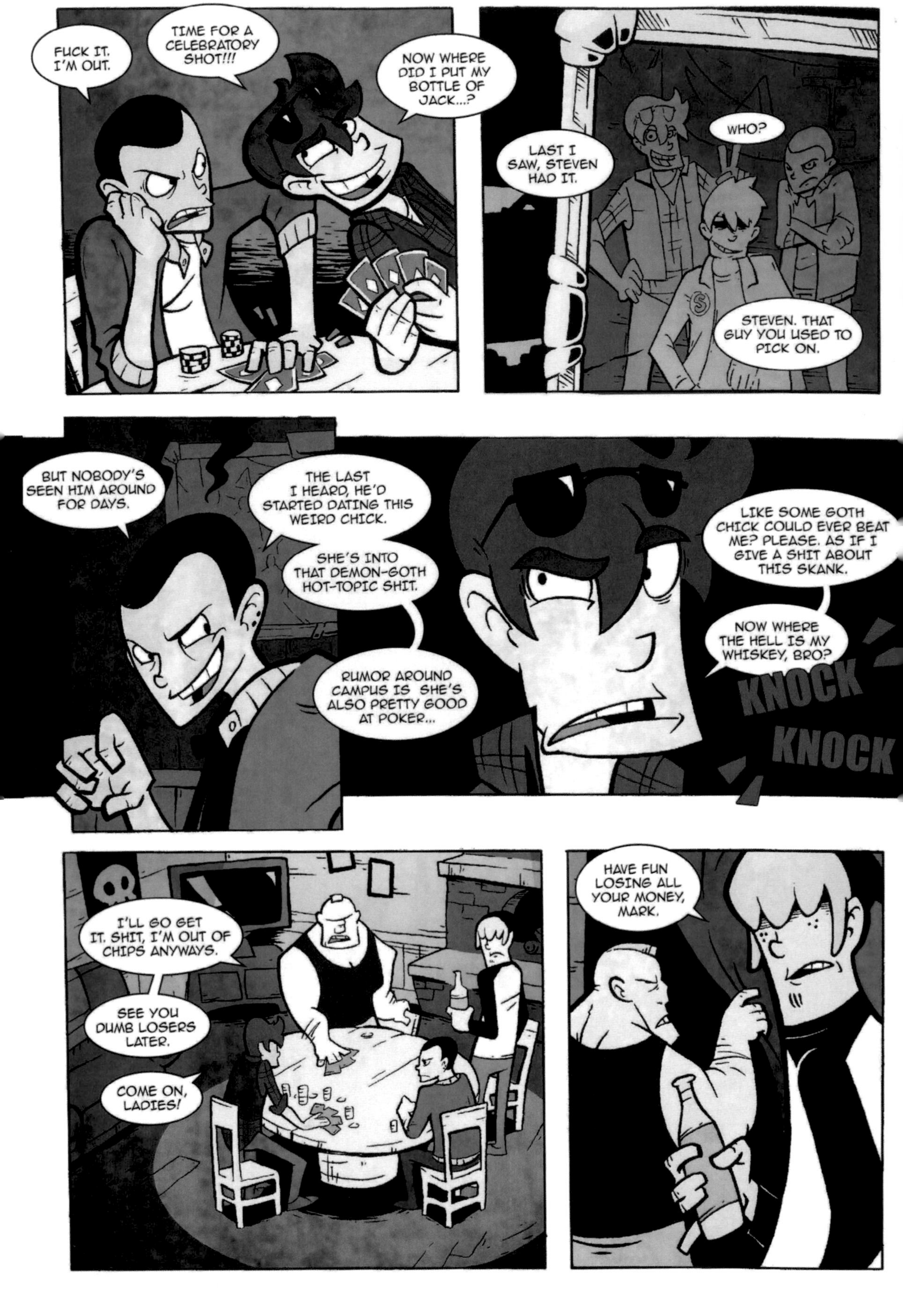
FUCK IT. I'M OUT.
TIME FOR A CELEBRATORY SHOT!!!
NOW WHERE DID I PUT MY BOTTLE OF JACK...?
LAST I SAW, STEVEN HAD IT.
WHO?
STEVEN. THAT GUY YOU USED TO PICK ON.
BUT NOBODY'S SEEN HIM AROUND FOR DAYS.
THE LAST I HEARD, HE'D STARTED DATING THIS WEIRD CHICK.
SHE'S INTO THAT DEMON-GOTH HOT-TOPIC SHIT.
RUMOR AROUND CAMPUS IS SHE'S ALSO PRETTY GOOD AT POKER...
LIKE SOME GOTH CHICK COULD EVER BEAT ME? PLEASE. AS IF I GIVE A SHIT ABOUT THIS SKANK.
NOW WHERE THE HELL IS MY WHISKEY, BRO?
KNOCK
KNOCK
I'LL GO GET IT. SHIT, I'M OUT OF CHIPS ANYWAYS.
SEE YOU DUMB LOSERS LATER.
COME ON, LADIES!
HAVE FUN LOSING ALL YOUR MONEY, MARK.

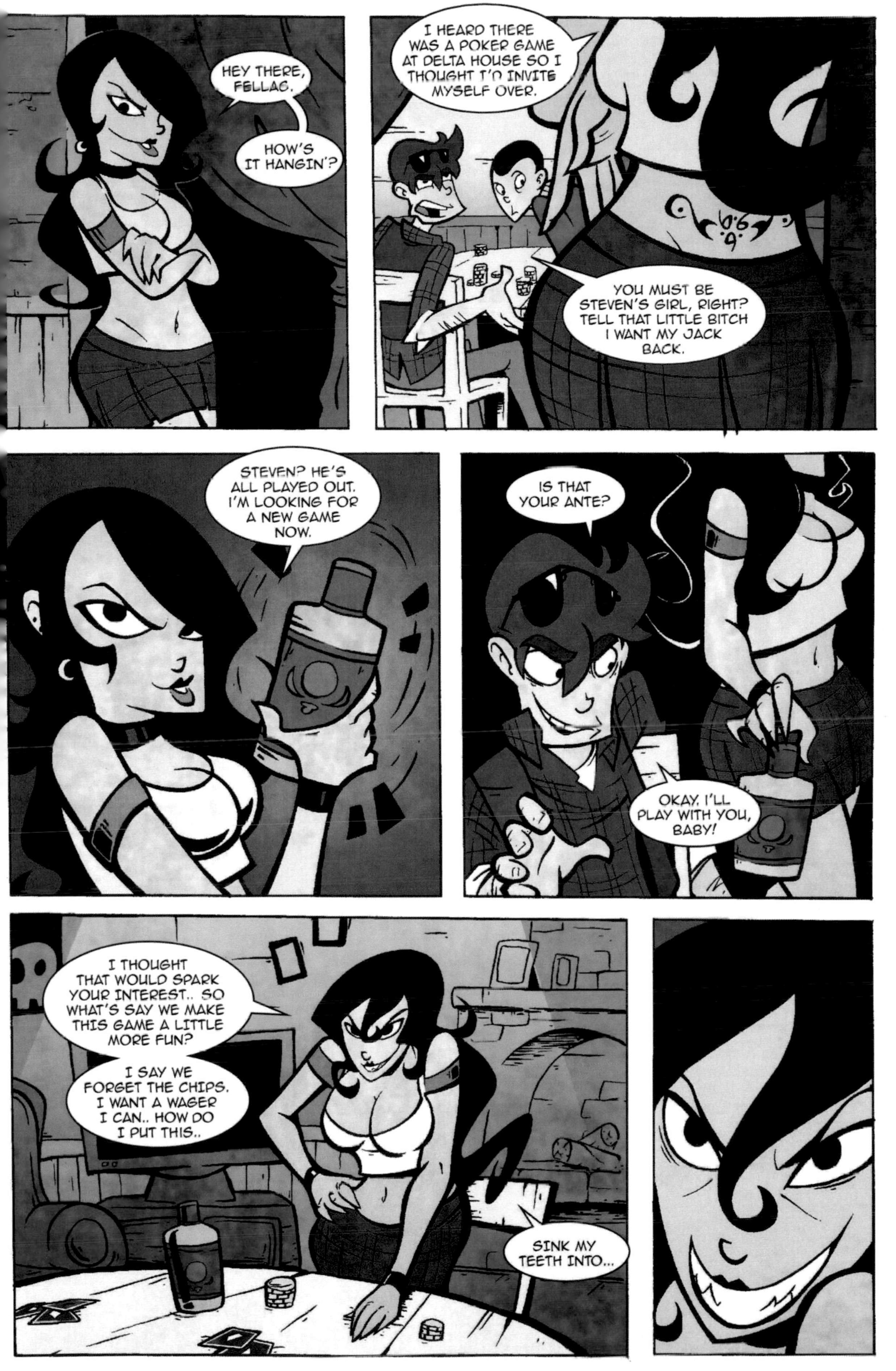
HEY THERE, FELLAS.
HOW'S IT HANGIN'?
I HEARD THERE WAS A POKER GAME AT DELTA HOUSE SO I THOUGHT I'D INVITE MYSELF OVER.
YOU MUST BE STEVEN'S GIRL, RIGHT? TELL THAT LITTLE BITCH I WANT MY JACK BACK.
STEVEN? HE'S ALL PLAYED OUT. I'M LOOKING FOR A NEW GAME NOW.
IS THAT YOUR ANTE?
OKAY, I'LL PLAY WITH YOU, BABY!
I THOUGHT THAT WOULD SPARK YOUR INTEREST.. SO WHAT'S SAY WE MAKE THIS GAME A LITTLE MORE FUN?
I SAY WE FORGET THE CHIPS. I WANT A WAGER I CAN.. HOW DO I PUT THIS..
SINK MY TEETH INTO...

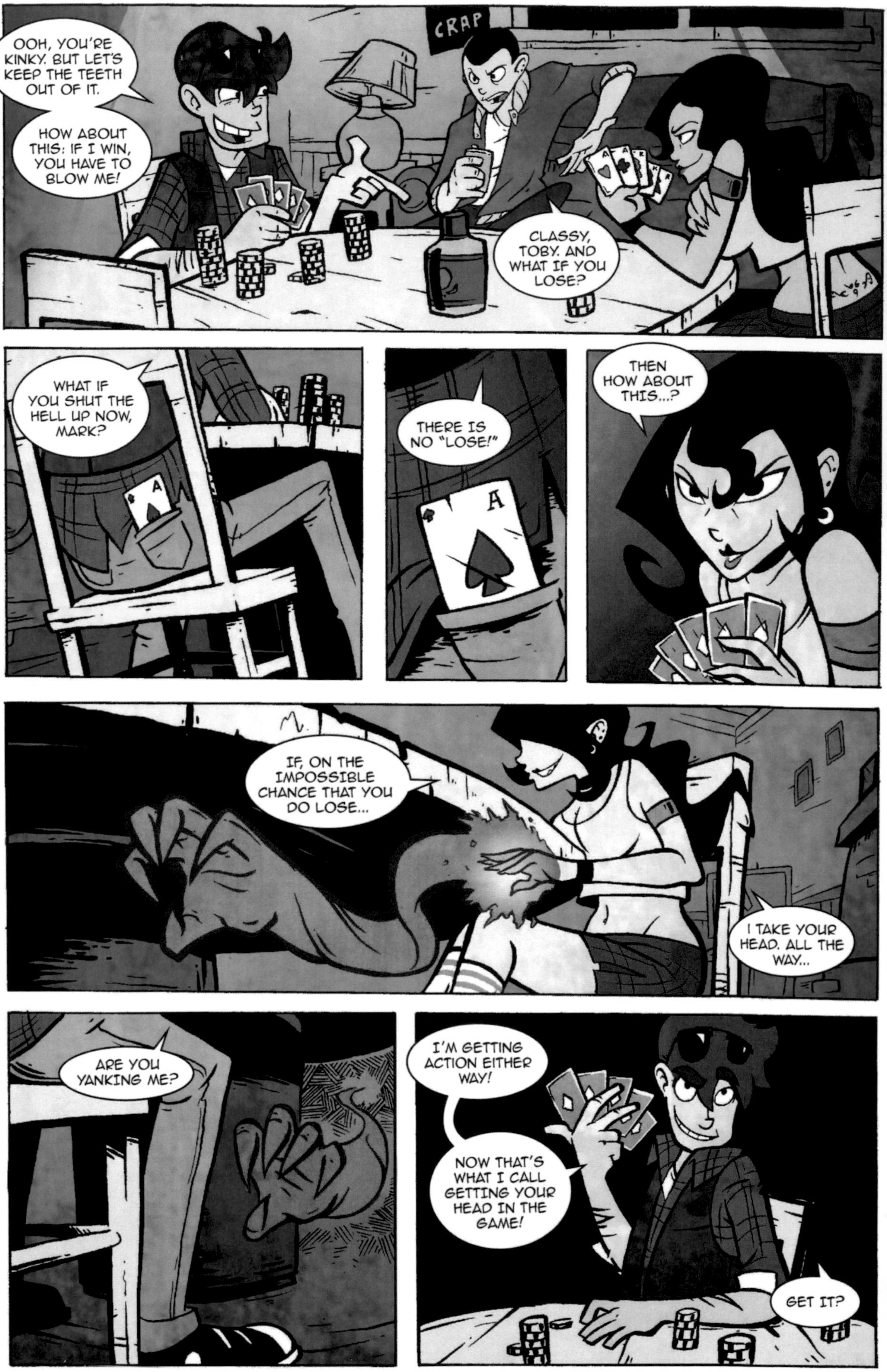
CRAP
OOH, YOU'RE KINKY. BUT LET'S KEEP THE TEETH OUT OF IT.
HOW ABOUT THIS: IF I WIN, YOU HAVE TO BLOW ME!
CLASSY, TOBY. AND WHAT IF YOU LOSE?
WHAT IF YOU SHUT THE HELL UP NOW, MARK?
THERE IS NO "LOSE!"
THEN HOW ABOUT THIS...?
IF, ON THE IMPOSSIBLE CHANCE THAT YOU DO LOSE...
I TAKE YOUR HEAD. ALL THE WAY...
ARE YOU YANKING ME?
I'M GETTING ACTION EITHER WAY!
NOW THAT'S WHAT I CALL GETTING YOUR HEAD IN THE GAME!
GET IT?

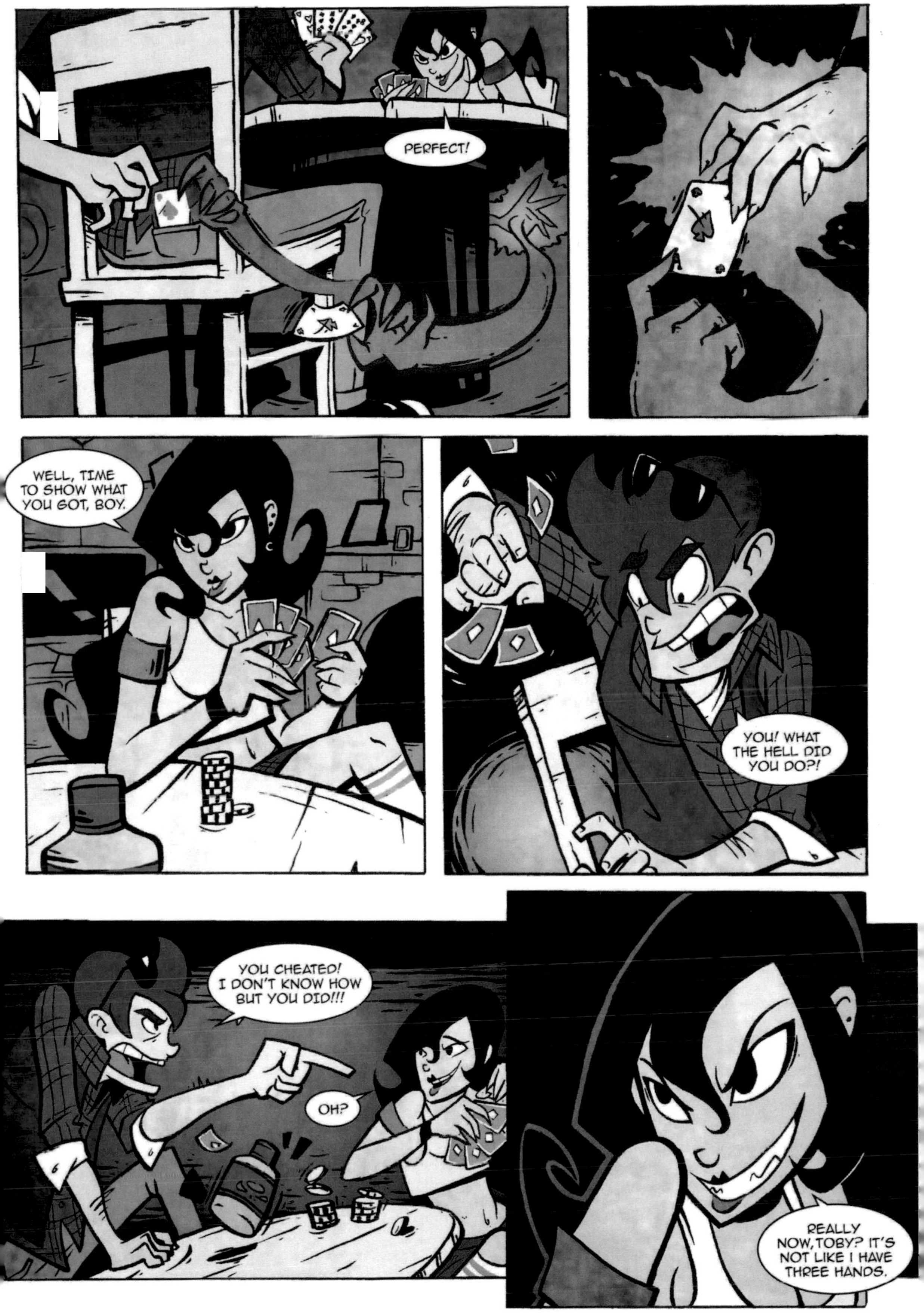
PERFECT!
WELL, TIME TO SHOW WHAT YOU GOT, BOY.
YOU! WHAT THE HELL DID YOU DO?!
YOU CHEATED! I DON'T KNOW HOW BUT YOU DID!!!
OH?
REALLY NOW, TOBY? IT'S NOT LIKE I HAVE THREE HANDS.

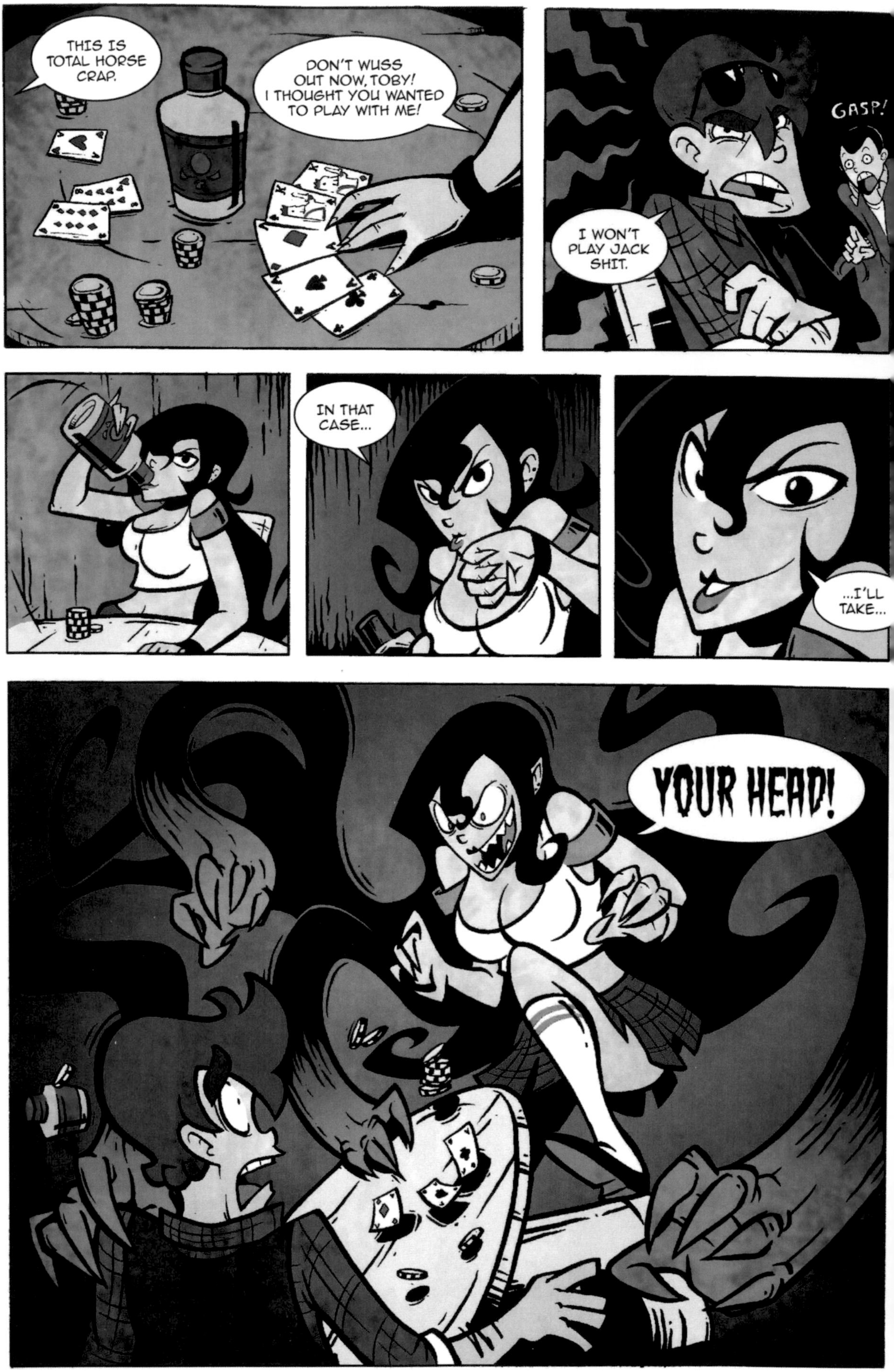
THIS IS TOTAL HORSE CRAP.
DON'T WUSS OUT NOW, TOBY! I THOUGHT YOU WANTED TO PLAY WITH ME!
I WON'T PLAY JACK SHIT.
GASP!
IN THAT CASE...
...I'LL TAKE...
YOUR HEAD!

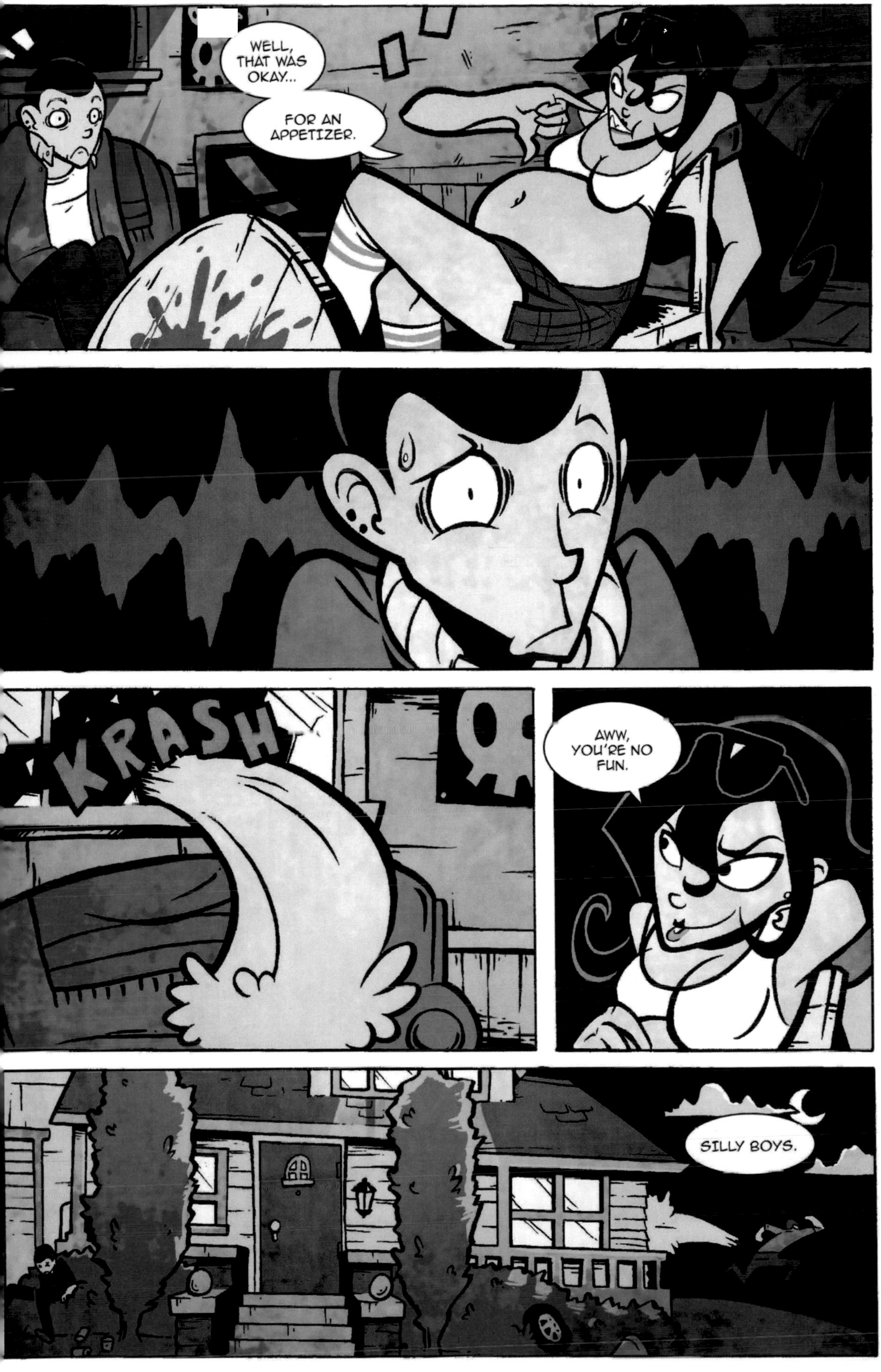
WELL, THAT WAS OKAY...
FOR AN APPETIZER.
KRASH
AWW, YOU'RE NO FUN.
SILLY BOYS.

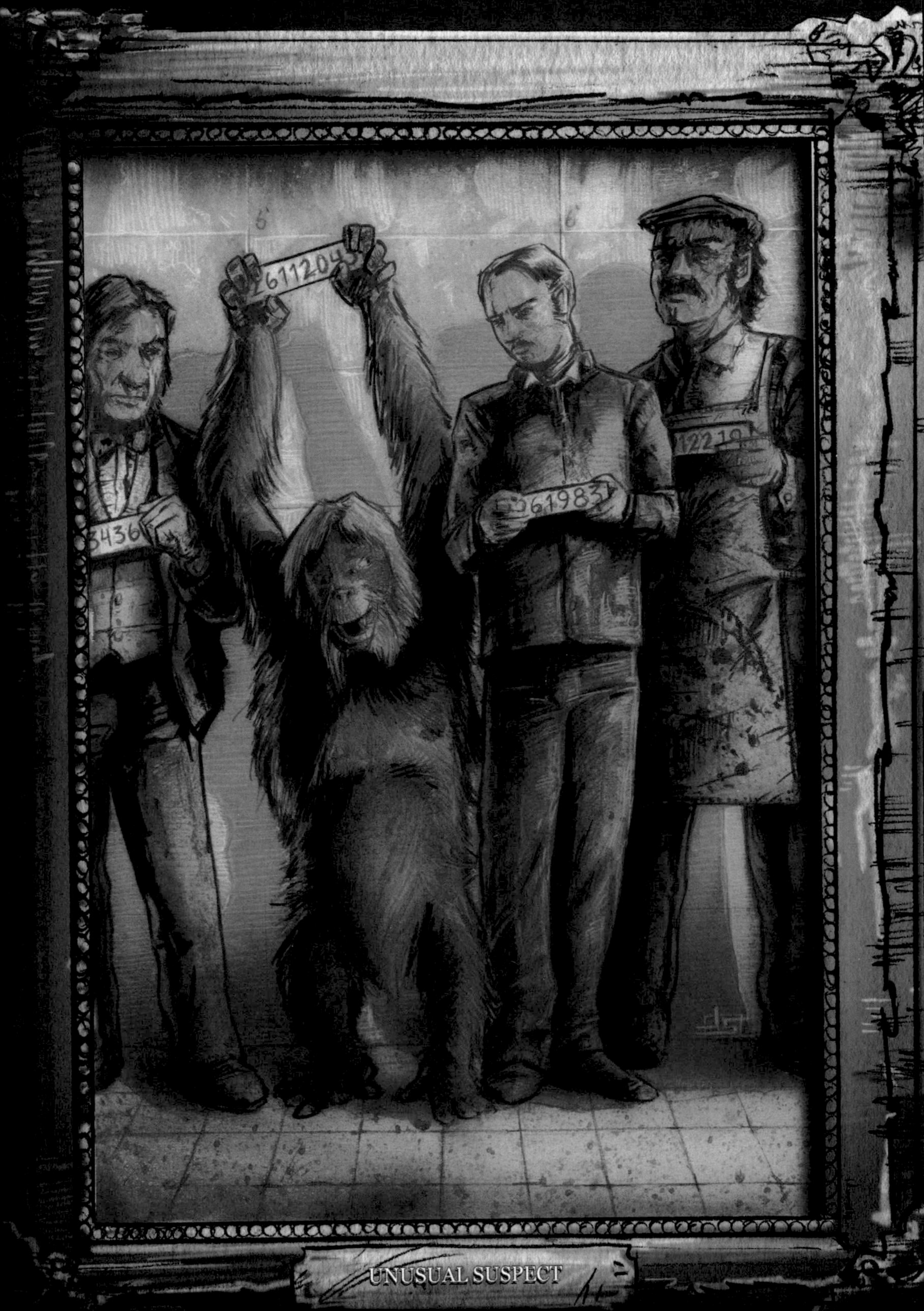
3436
61983

UNUSUAL SUSPECT

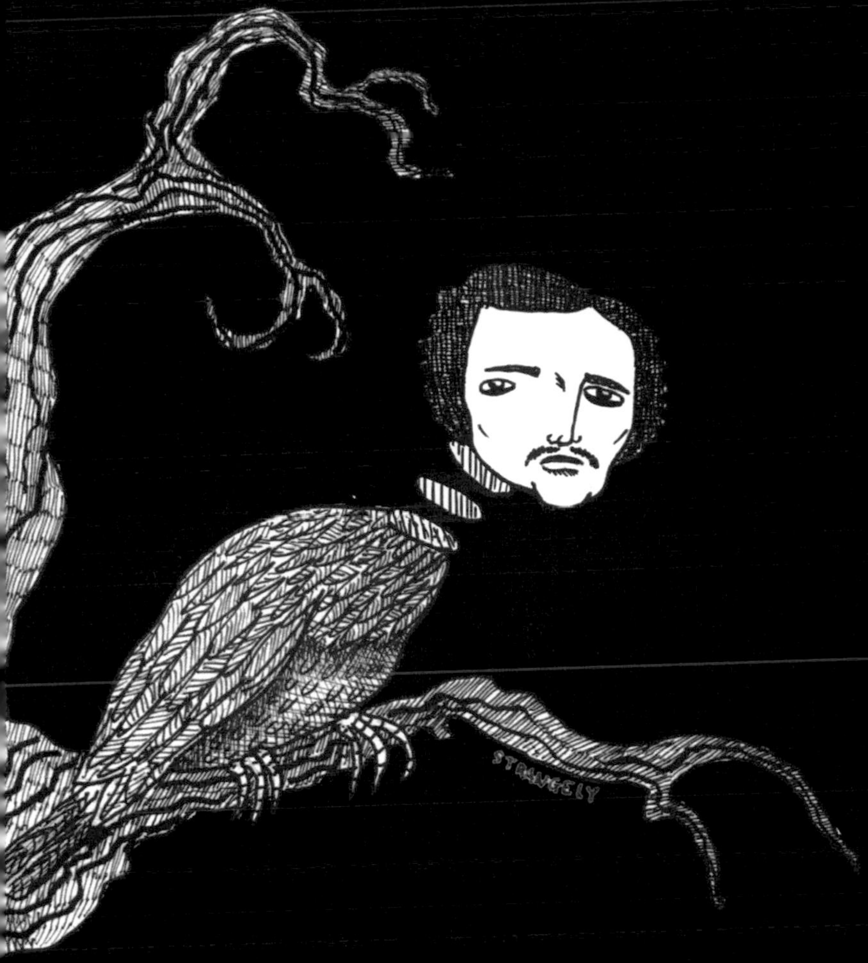
STRANGELY

BUT HE GREW OLD -
THIS KNIGHT SO BOLD -
AND O'ER HIS HEART A SHADOW
FELL AS HE FOUND
NO SPOT OF GROUND
THAT LOOKED LIKE ELDORADO.

AND, AS HIS STRENGTH
FAILED HIM AT LENGTH,
HE MET A PILGRIM SHADOW -
"SHADOW," SAID HE,
"WHERE CAN IT BE -
THIS LAND OF ELDORADO?"

from "ELDORADO"

ELDORADO

Written by Sherezada Windham-Kent
Art by Alex Cormack

OVER THE MOUNTAINS OF THE MOON...

...DOWN THE VALLEY OF THE SHADOW...

...RIDE, BOLDLY RIDE...

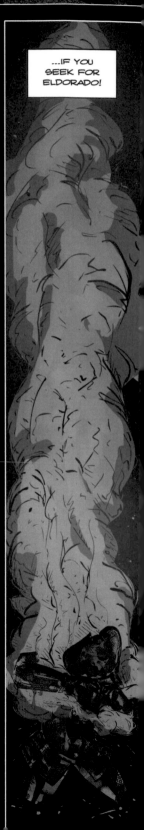

...IF YOU SEEK FOR ELDORADO!

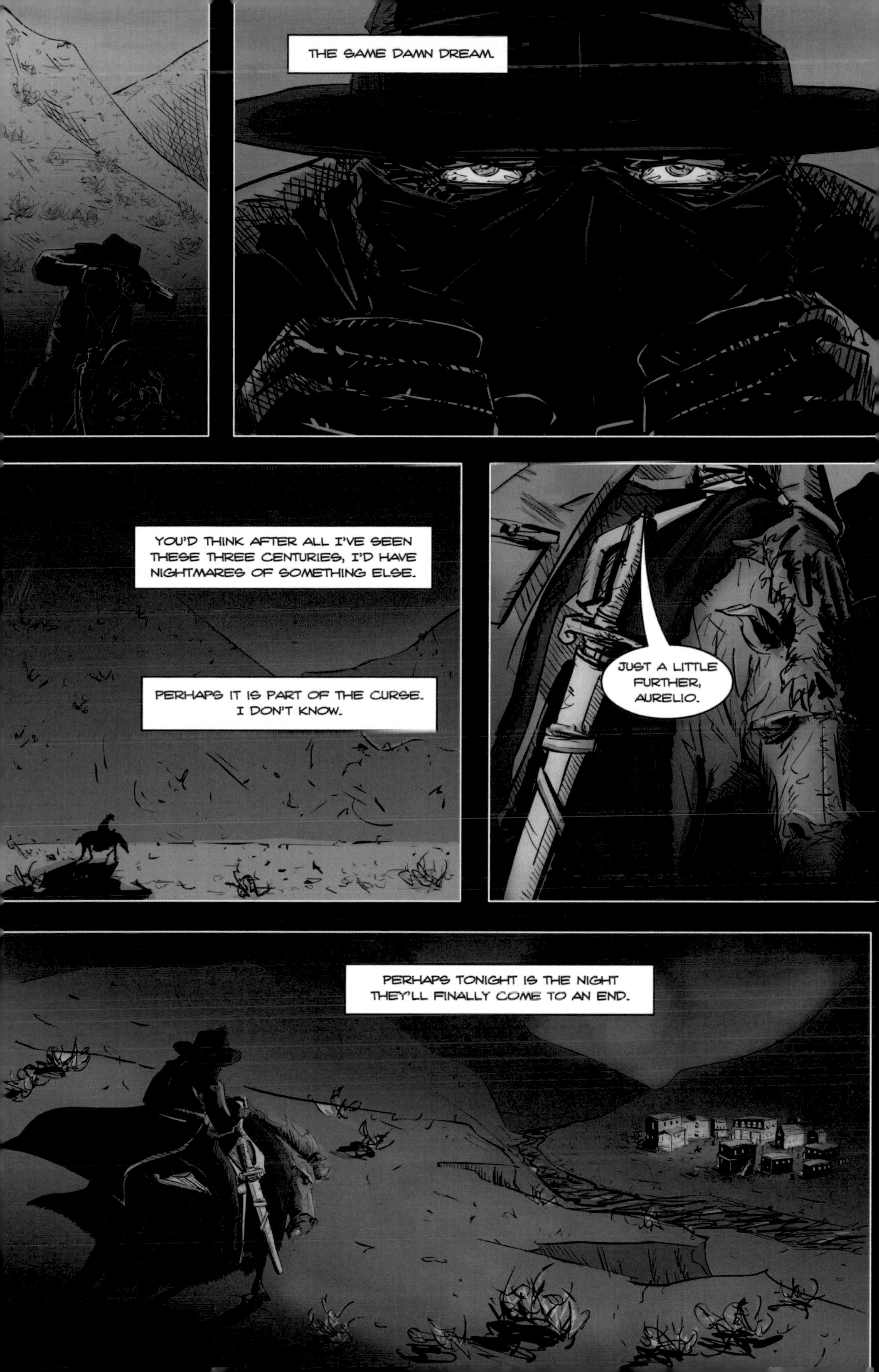
THE SAME DAMN DREAM.
YOU'D THINK AFTER ALL I'VE SEEN THESE THREE CENTURIES, I'D HAVE NIGHTMARES OF SOMETHING ELSE.
PERHAPS IT IS PART OF THE CURSE. I DON'T KNOW.
JUST A LITTLE FURTHER, AURELIO.
PERHAPS TONIGHT IS THE NIGHT THEY'LL FINALLY COME TO AN END.

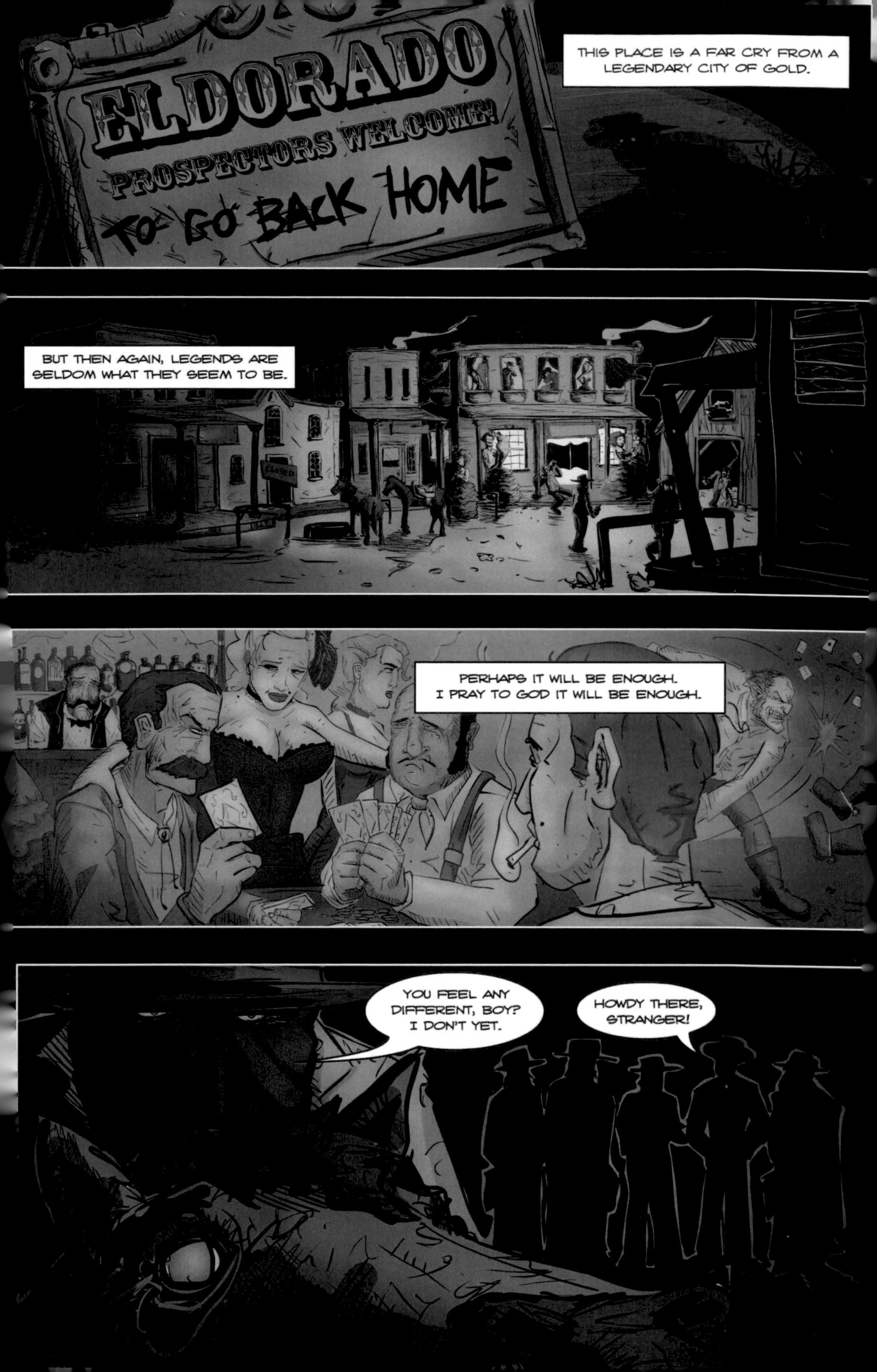
ELDORADO
PROSPECTORS WELCOME!
TO GO BACK HOME
THIS PLACE IS A FAR CRY FROM A LEGENDARY CITY OF GOLD.
BUT THEN AGAIN, LEGENDS ARE SELDOM WHAT THEY SEEM TO BE.
CLOSED
PERHAPS IT WILL BE ENOUGH. I PRAY TO GOD IT WILL BE ENOUGH.
YOU FEEL ANY DIFFERENT, BOY? I DON'T YET.
HOWDY THERE, STRANGER!

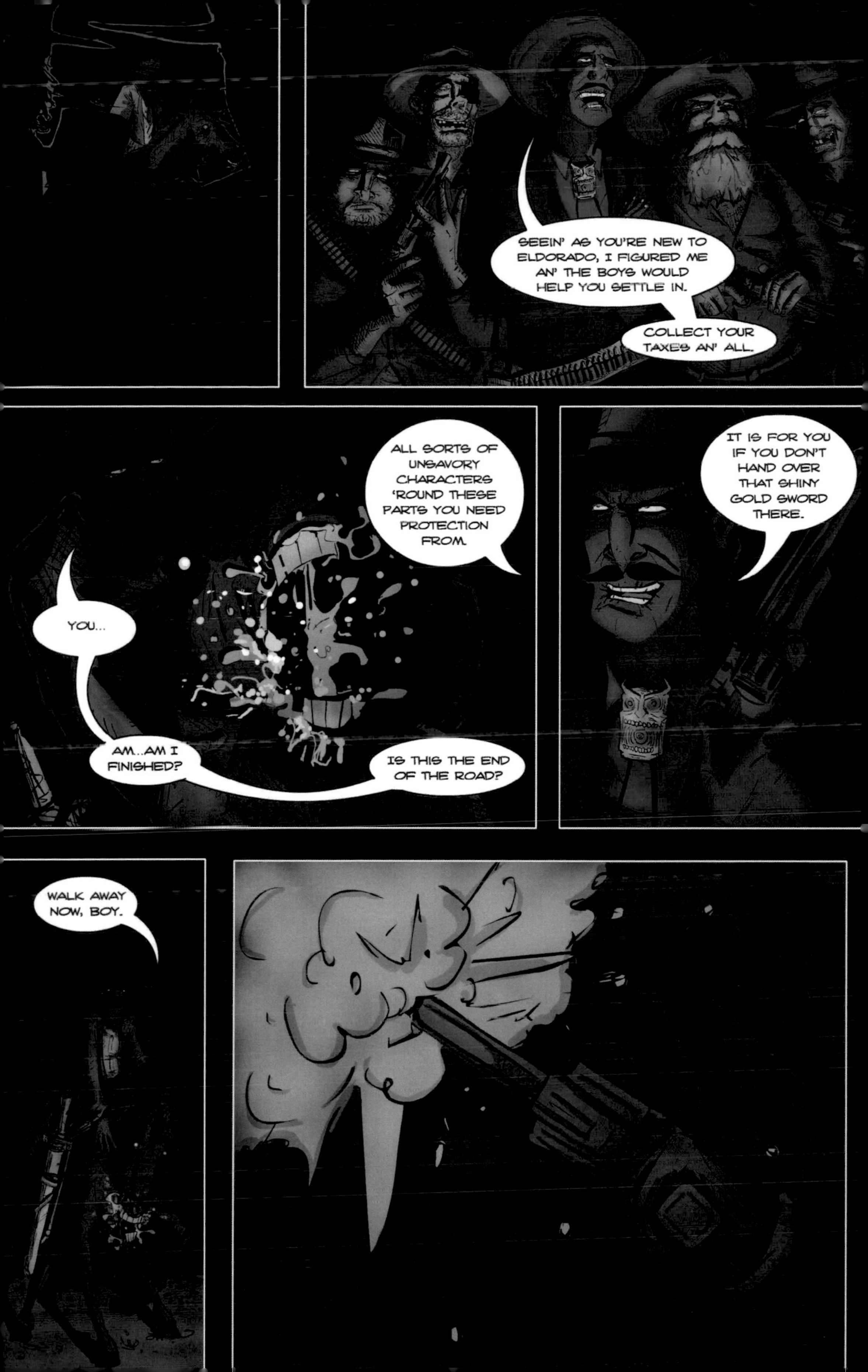
SEEIN' AS YOU'RE NEW TO ELDORADO, I FIGURED ME AN' THE BOYS WOULD HELP YOU SETTLE IN.
COLLECT YOUR TAXES AN' ALL.
ALL SORTS OF UNSAVORY CHARACTERS 'ROUND THESE PARTS YOU NEED PROTECTION FROM.
YOU...
AM...AM I FINISHED?
IS THIS THE END OF THE ROAD?
IT IS FOR YOU IF YOU DON'T HAND OVER THAT SHINY GOLD SWORD THERE.
WALK AWAY NOW, BOY.

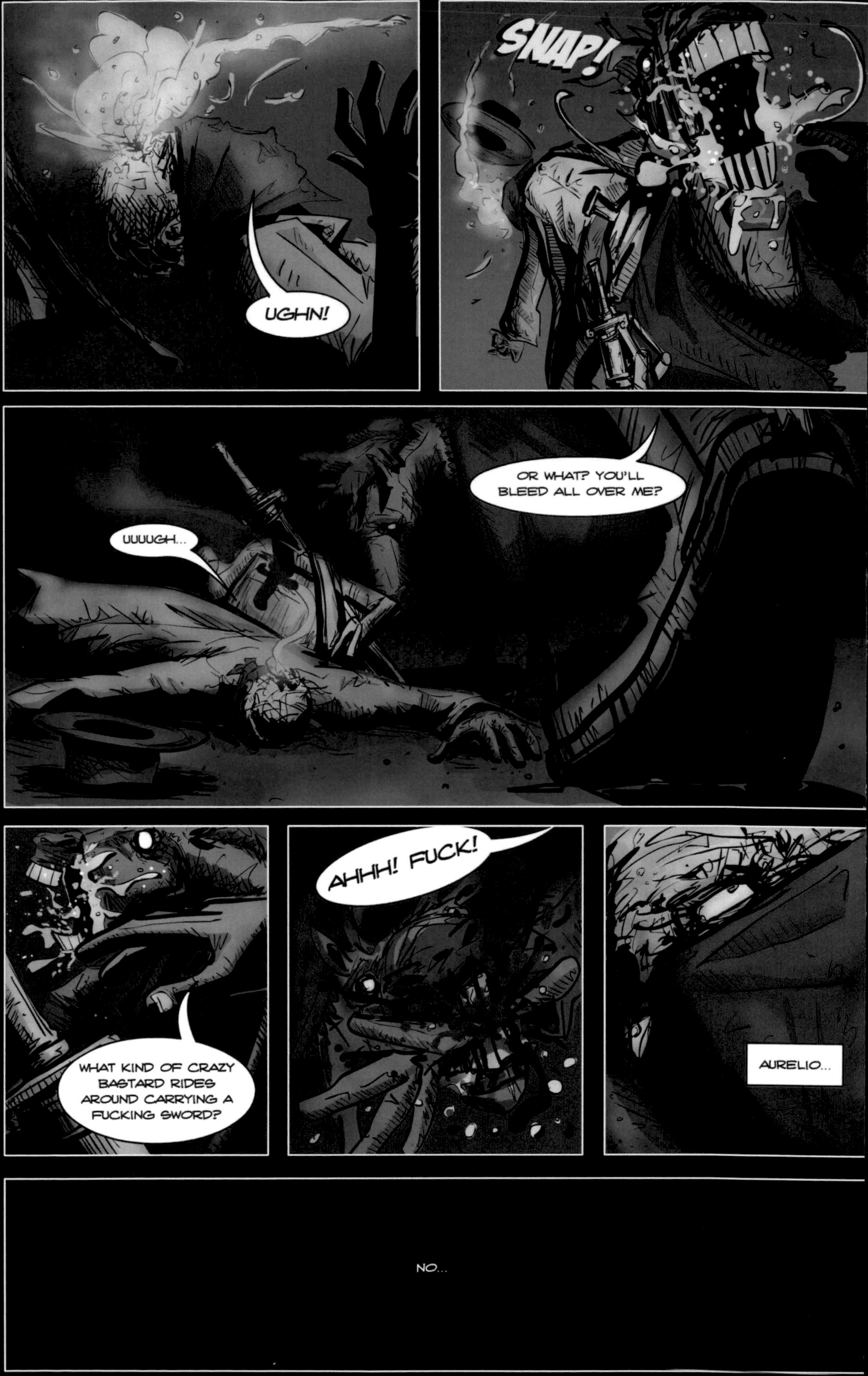

UGHN!
SNAP!
OR WHAT? YOU'LL BLEED ALL OVER ME?
UUUUGH...
WHAT KIND OF CRAZY BASTARD RIDES AROUND CARRYING A FUCKING SWORD?
AHHH! FUCK!
AURELIO...
NO...

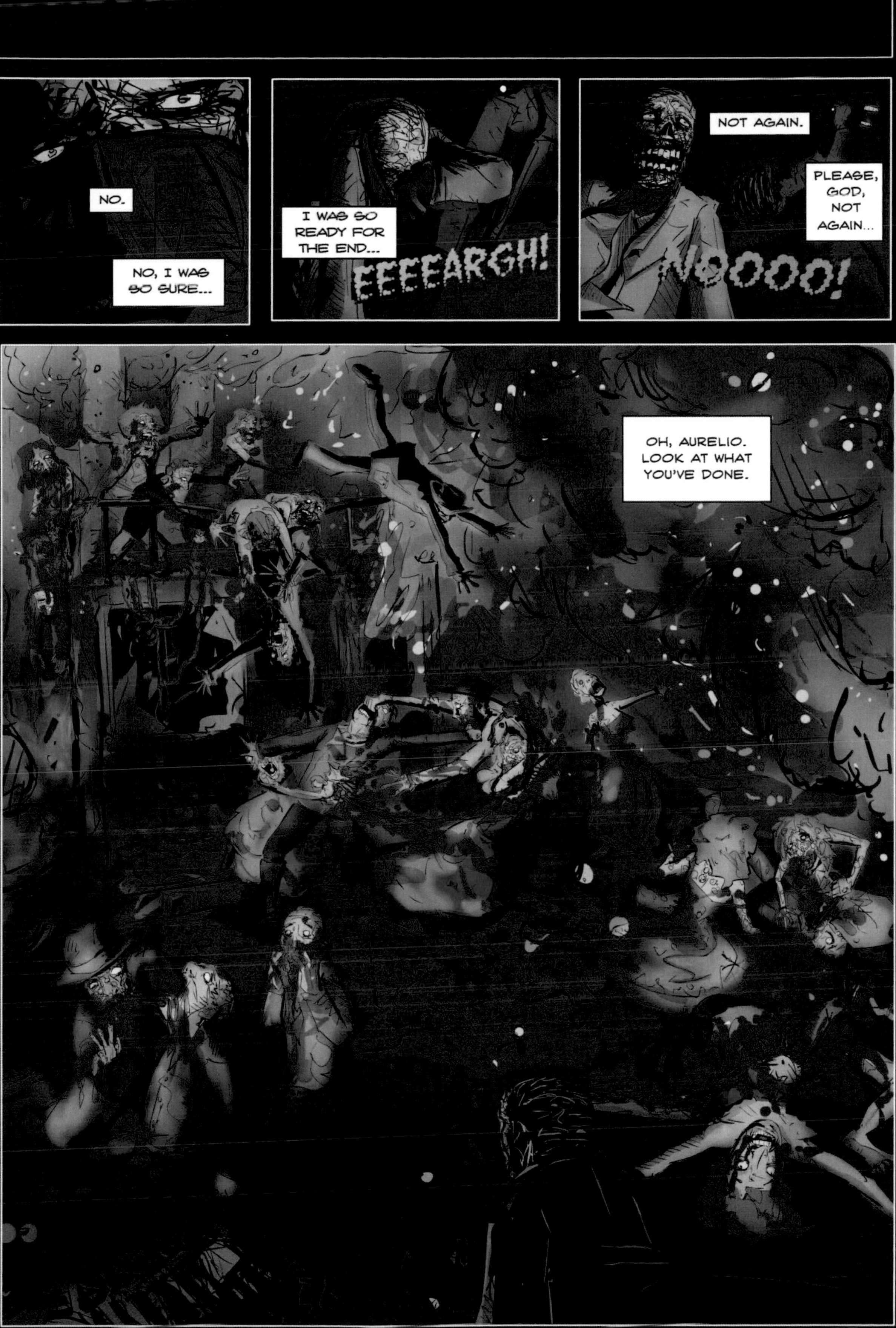
NO.
NO, I WAS SO SURE...
I WAS SO READY FOR THE END...
EEEEARGH!
NOT AGAIN.
PLEASE, GOD, NOT AGAIN...
NOOOOO!
OH, AURELIO. LOOK AT WHAT YOU'VE DONE.

BRUTE THOUGH YOU WERE, YOU DON'T DESERVE THIS FATE.

NONE OF YOU DO.

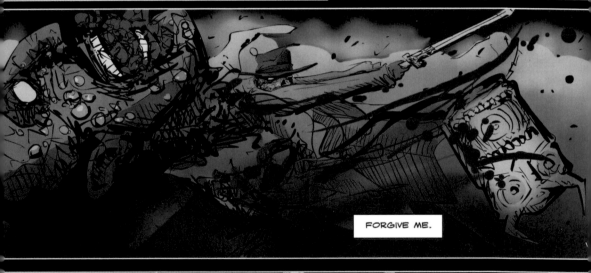

FORGIVE ME.

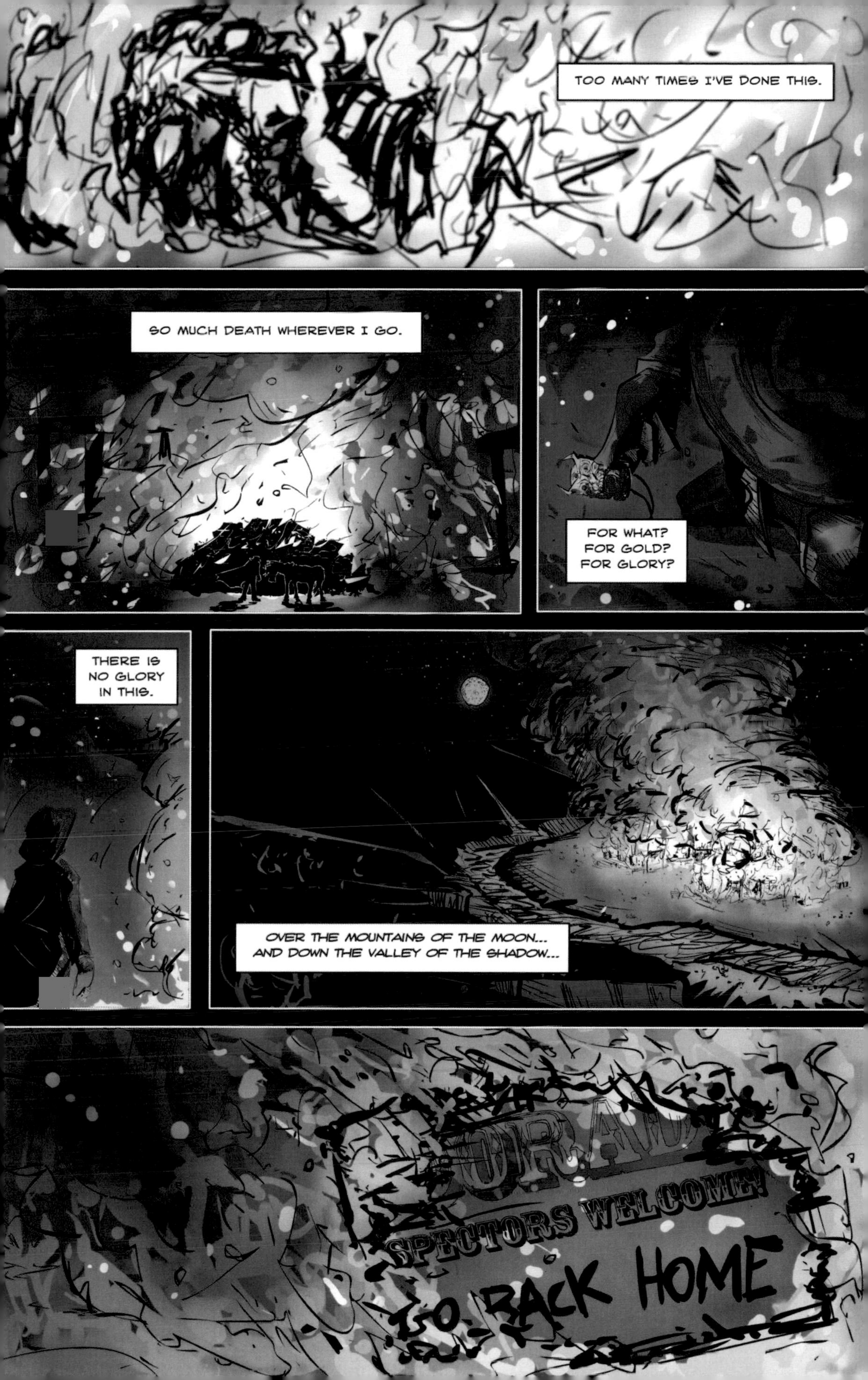
TOO MANY TIMES I'VE DONE THIS.
SO MUCH DEATH WHEREVER I GO.
FOR WHAT? FOR GOLD? FOR GLORY?
THERE IS NO GLORY IN THIS.
OVER THE MOUNTAINS OF THE MOON... AND DOWN THE VALLEY OF THE SHADOW...
SPECTORS WELCOME!
BACK HOME

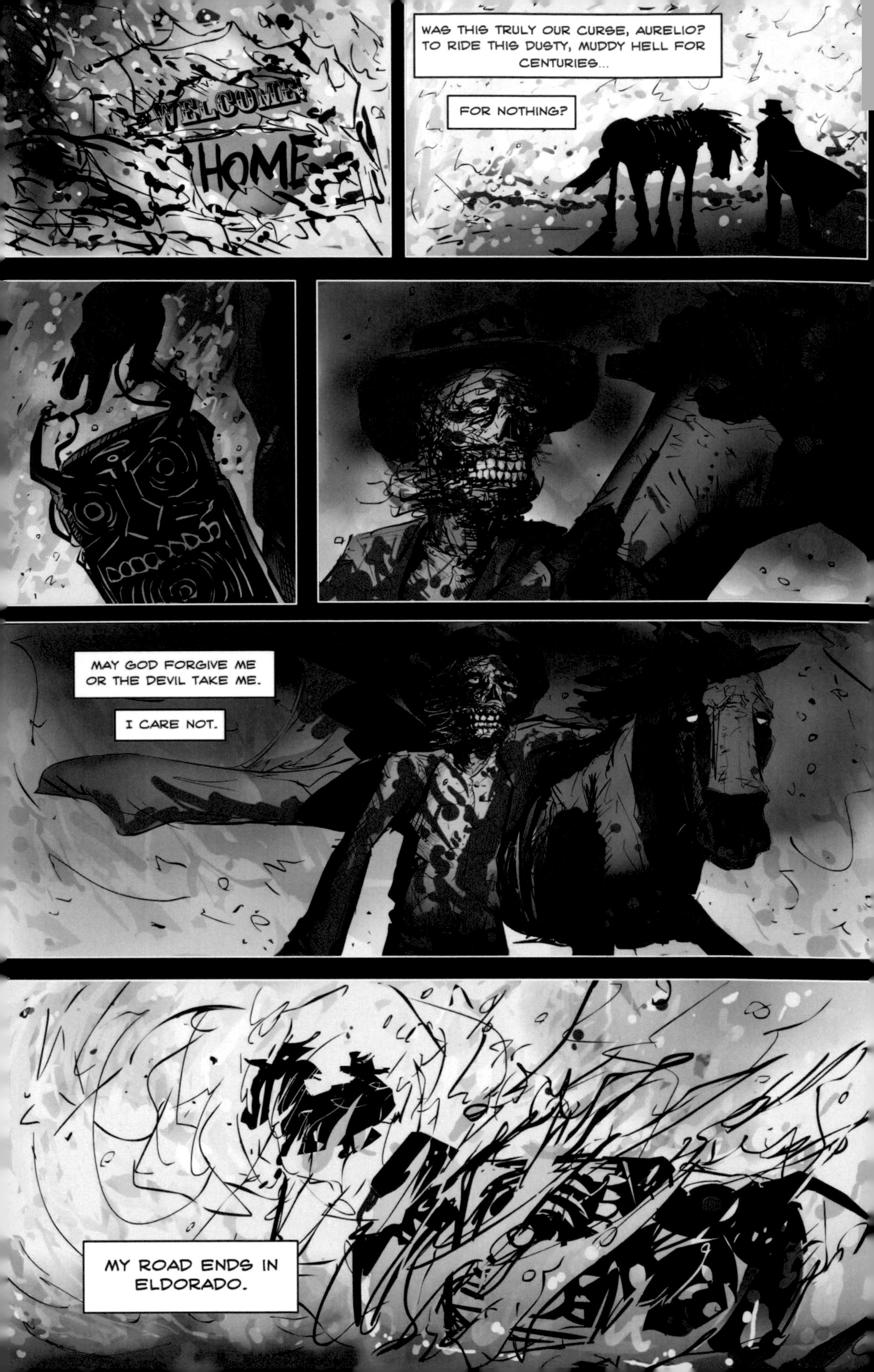
WELCOME
HOME
WAS THIS TRULY OUR CURSE, AURELIO? TO RIDE THIS DUSTY, MUDDY HELL FOR CENTURIES...
FOR NOTHING?
MAY GOD FORGIVE ME OR THE DEVIL TAKE ME.
I CARE NOT.
MY ROAD ENDS IN ELDORADO.

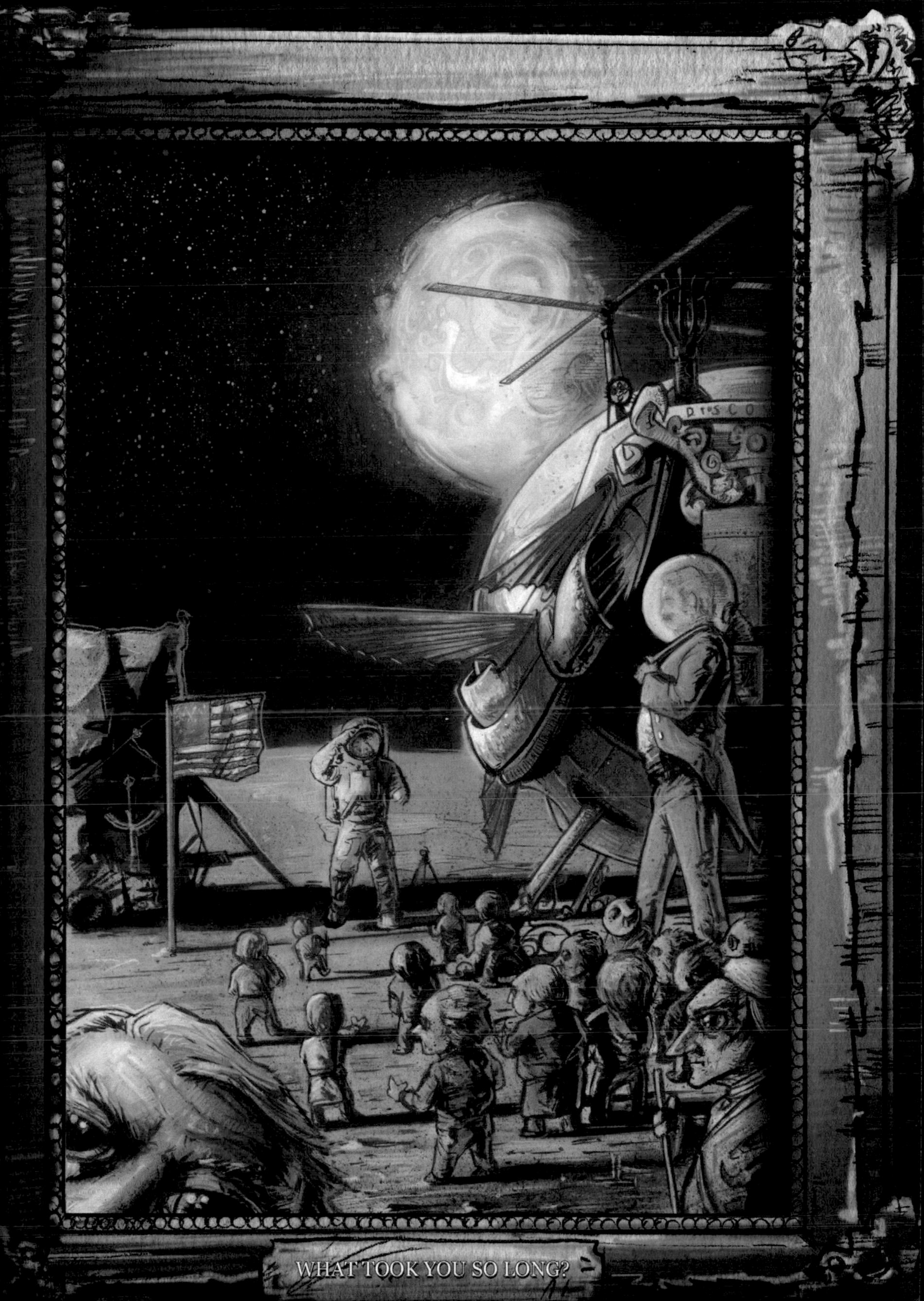
WHAT TOOK YOU SO LONG?

MRS. W. WAS A LITTLE INDISPOSED, AND WOULD DECLINE COMING
ON BOARD UNTIL TO-MORROW, AT THE HOUR OF SAILING.

from "THE OBLONG BOX"

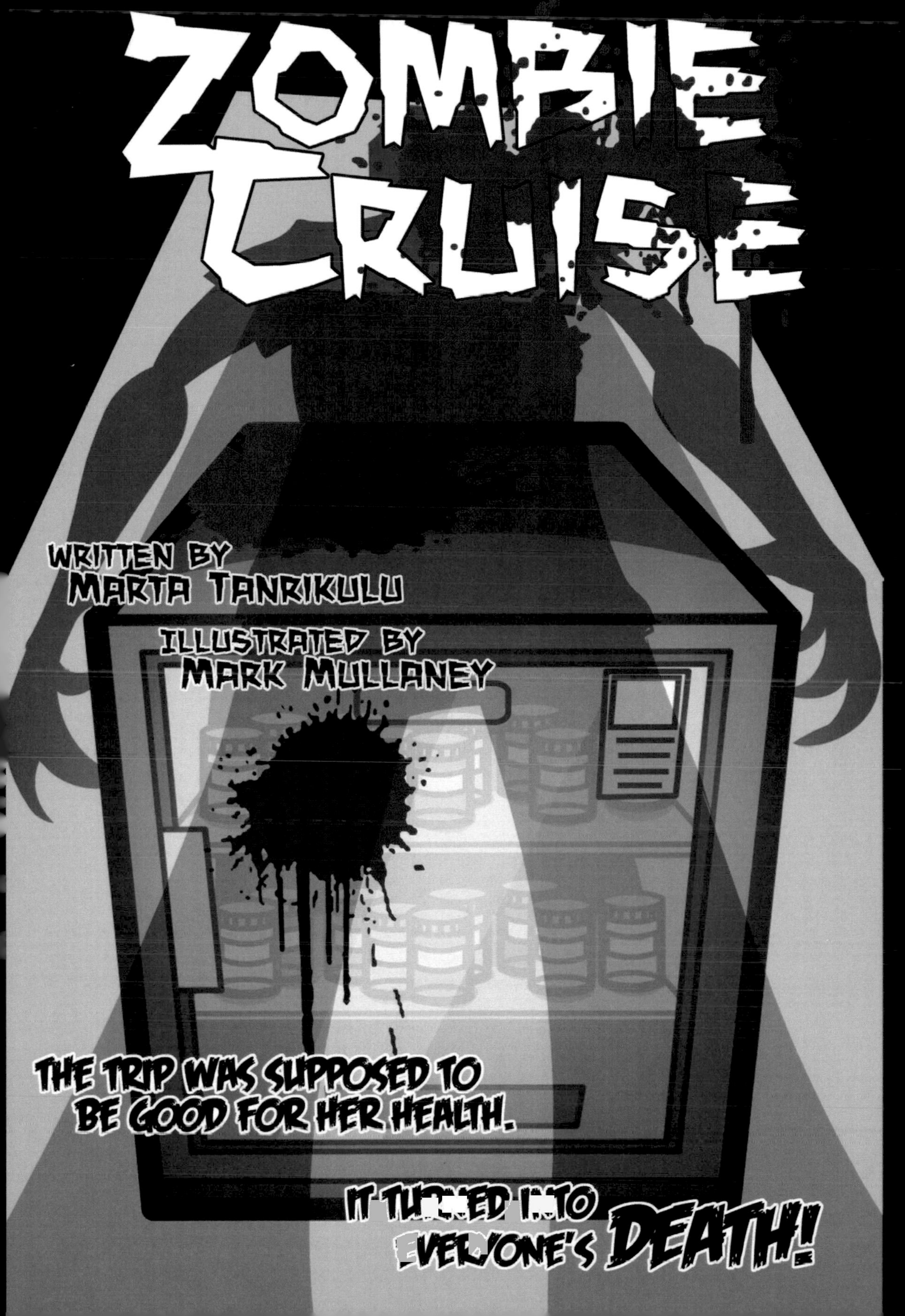
ZOMBIE CRUISE
WRITTEN BY
MARTA TANRIKULU
ILLUSTRATED BY
MARK MULLANEY
THE TRIP WAS SUPPOSED TO BE GOOD FOR HER HEALTH.
IT TURNED INTO EVERYONE'S DEATH!

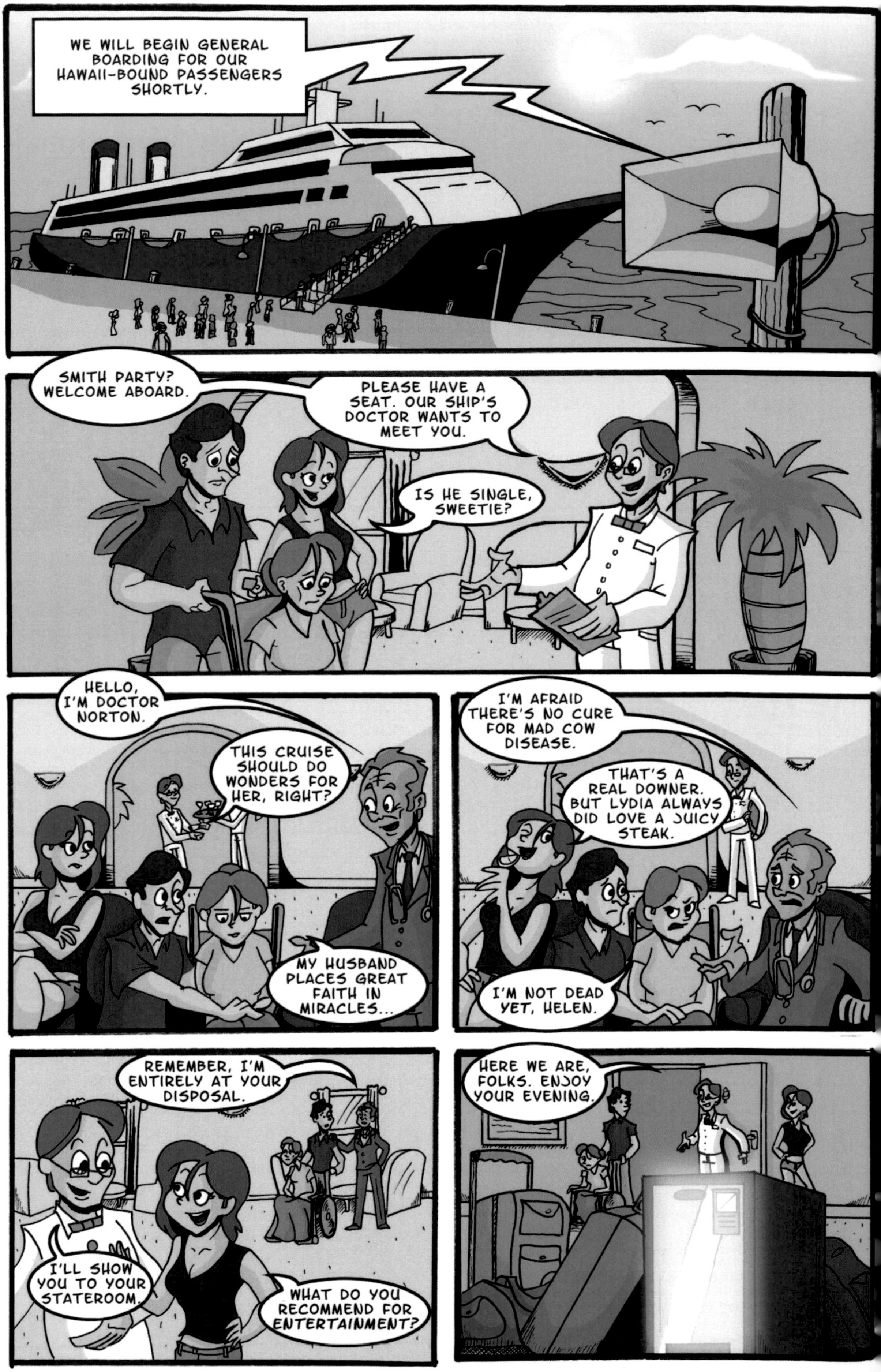
WE WILL BEGIN GENERAL BOARDING FOR OUR HAWAII-BOUND PASSENGERS SHORTLY.
SMITH PARTY? WELCOME ABOARD.
PLEASE HAVE A SEAT. OUR SHIP'S DOCTOR WANTS TO MEET YOU.
IS HE SINGLE, SWEETIE?
HELLO, I'M DOCTOR NORTON.
THIS CRUISE SHOULD DO WONDERS FOR HER, RIGHT?
MY HUSBAND PLACES GREAT FAITH IN MIRACLES...
I'M AFRAID THERE'S NO CURE FOR MAD COW DISEASE.
THAT'S A REAL DOWNER. BUT LYDIA ALWAYS DID LOVE A JUICY STEAK.
I'M NOT DEAD YET, HELEN.
REMEMBER, I'M ENTIRELY AT YOUR DISPOSAL.
I'LL SHOW YOU TO YOUR STATEROOM.
WHAT DO YOU RECOMMEND FOR ENTERTAINMENT?
HERE WE ARE, FOLKS. ENJOY YOUR EVENING.

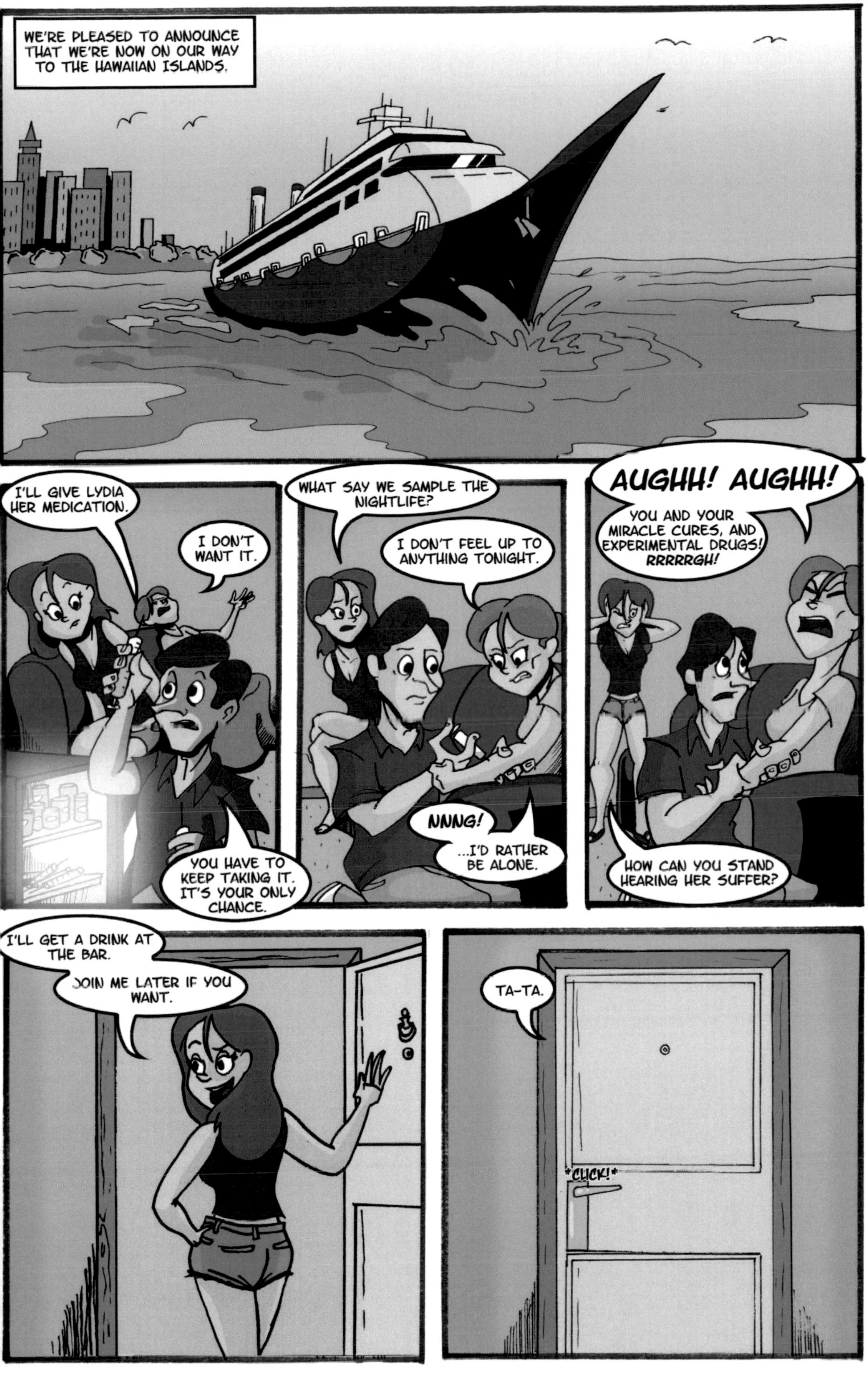
WE'RE PLEASED TO ANNOUNCE THAT WE'RE NOW ON OUR WAY TO THE HAWAIIAN ISLANDS.
I'LL GIVE LYDIA HER MEDICATION.
I DON'T WANT IT.
YOU HAVE TO KEEP TAKING IT. IT'S YOUR ONLY CHANCE.
WHAT SAY WE SAMPLE THE NIGHTLIFE?
I DON'T FEEL UP TO ANYTHING TONIGHT.
NNNG!
...I'D RATHER BE ALONE.
AUGHH! AUGHH!
YOU AND YOUR MIRACLE CURES, AND EXPERIMENTAL DRUGS! RRRRRGH!
HOW CAN YOU STAND HEARING HER SUFFER?
I'LL GET A DRINK AT THE BAR.
JOIN ME LATER IF YOU WANT.
TA-TA.
CLICK!

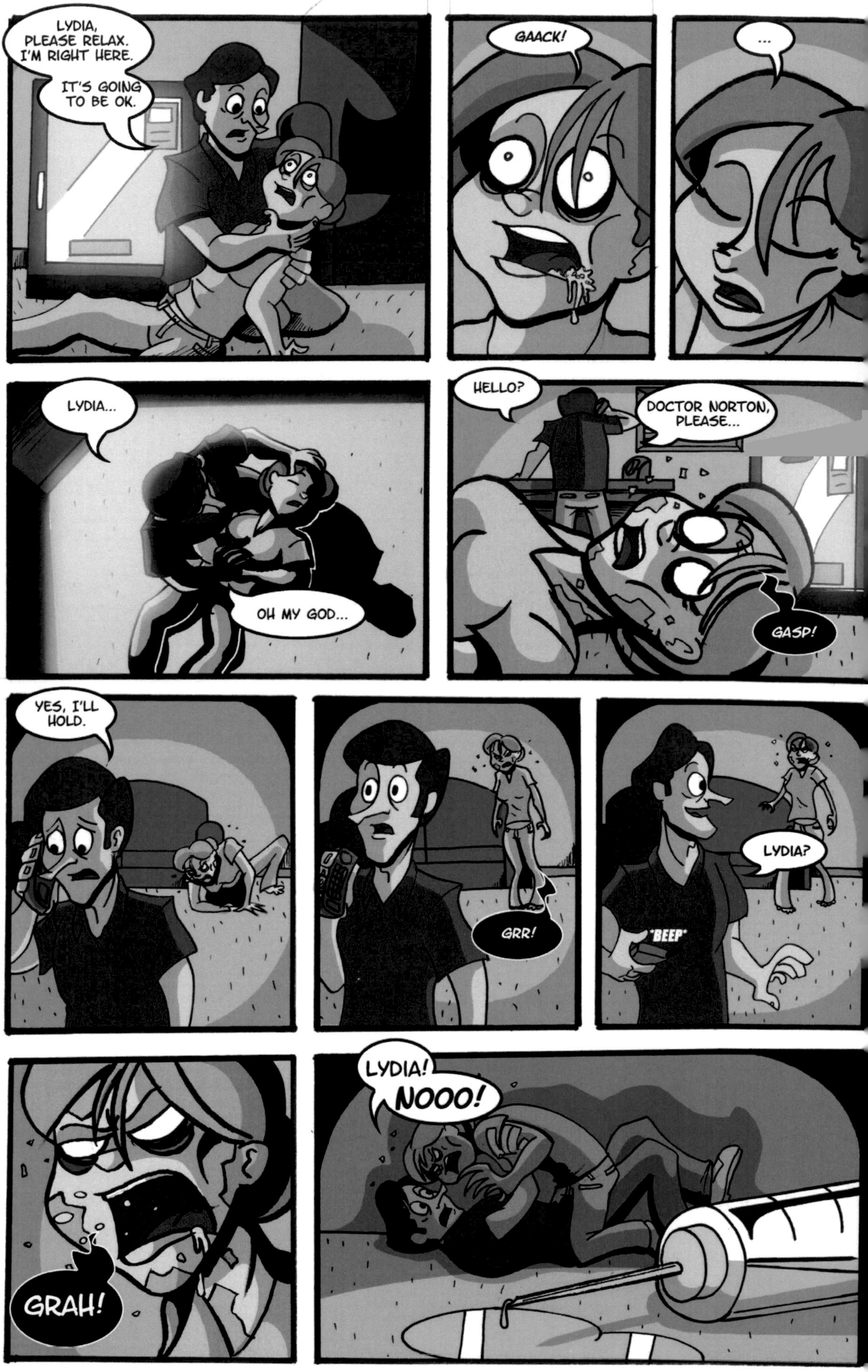
LYDIA, PLEASE RELAX. I'M RIGHT HERE.
IT'S GOING TO BE OK.
GAACK!
...
LYDIA...
OH MY GOD...
HELLO?
DOCTOR NORTON, PLEASE...
GASP!
YES, I'LL HOLD.
GRR!
LYDIA?
BEEP
GRAH!
LYDIA!
NOOO!

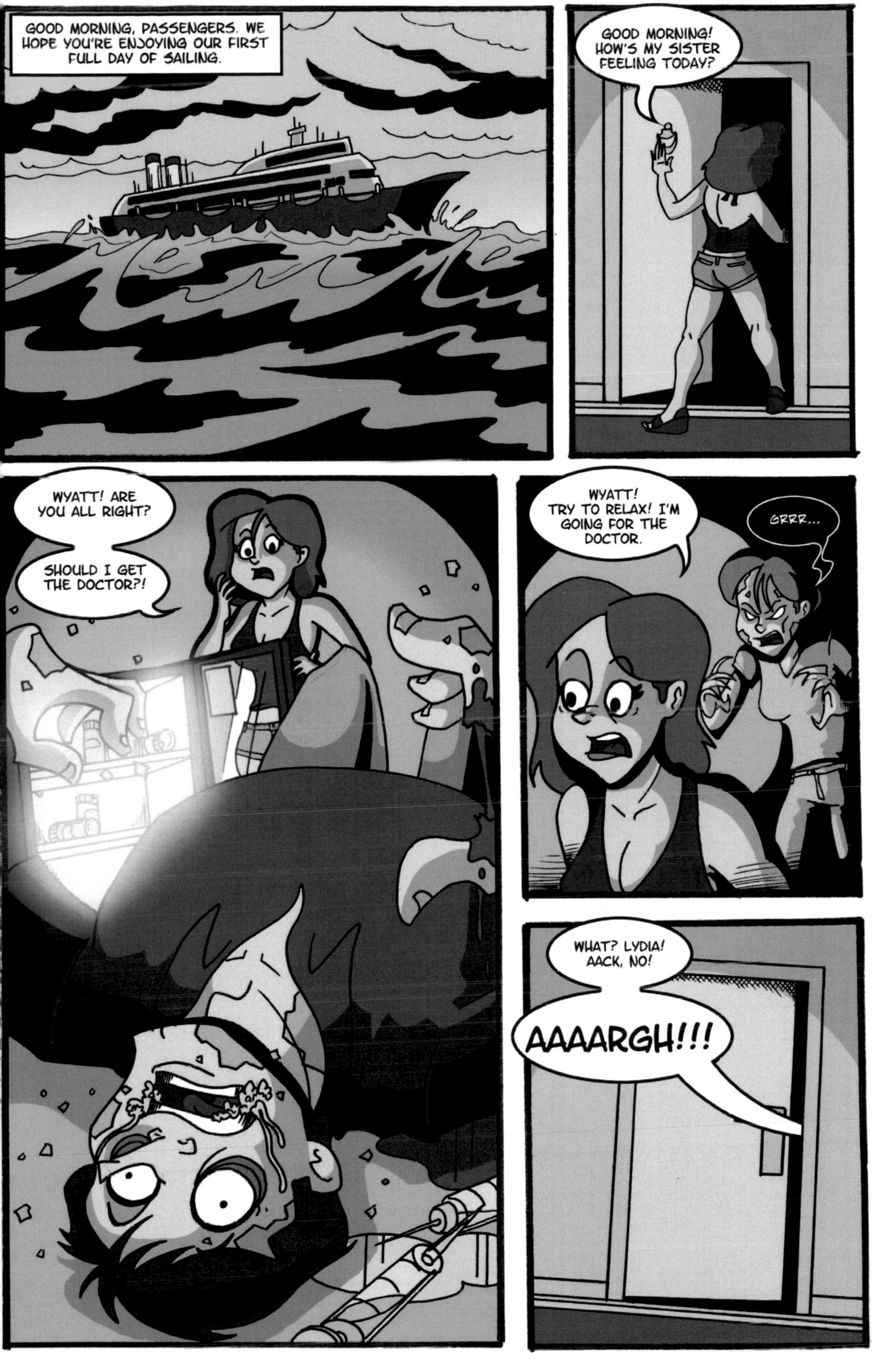
GOOD MORNING, PASSENGERS. WE HOPE YOU'RE ENJOYING OUR FIRST FULL DAY OF SAILING.
GOOD MORNING! HOW'S MY SISTER FEELING TODAY?
WYATT! ARE YOU ALL RIGHT?
SHOULD I GET THE DOCTOR?!
WYATT! TRY TO RELAX! I'M GOING FOR THE DOCTOR.
GRRR...
WHAT? LYDIA! AACK, NO!
AAAARGH!!!

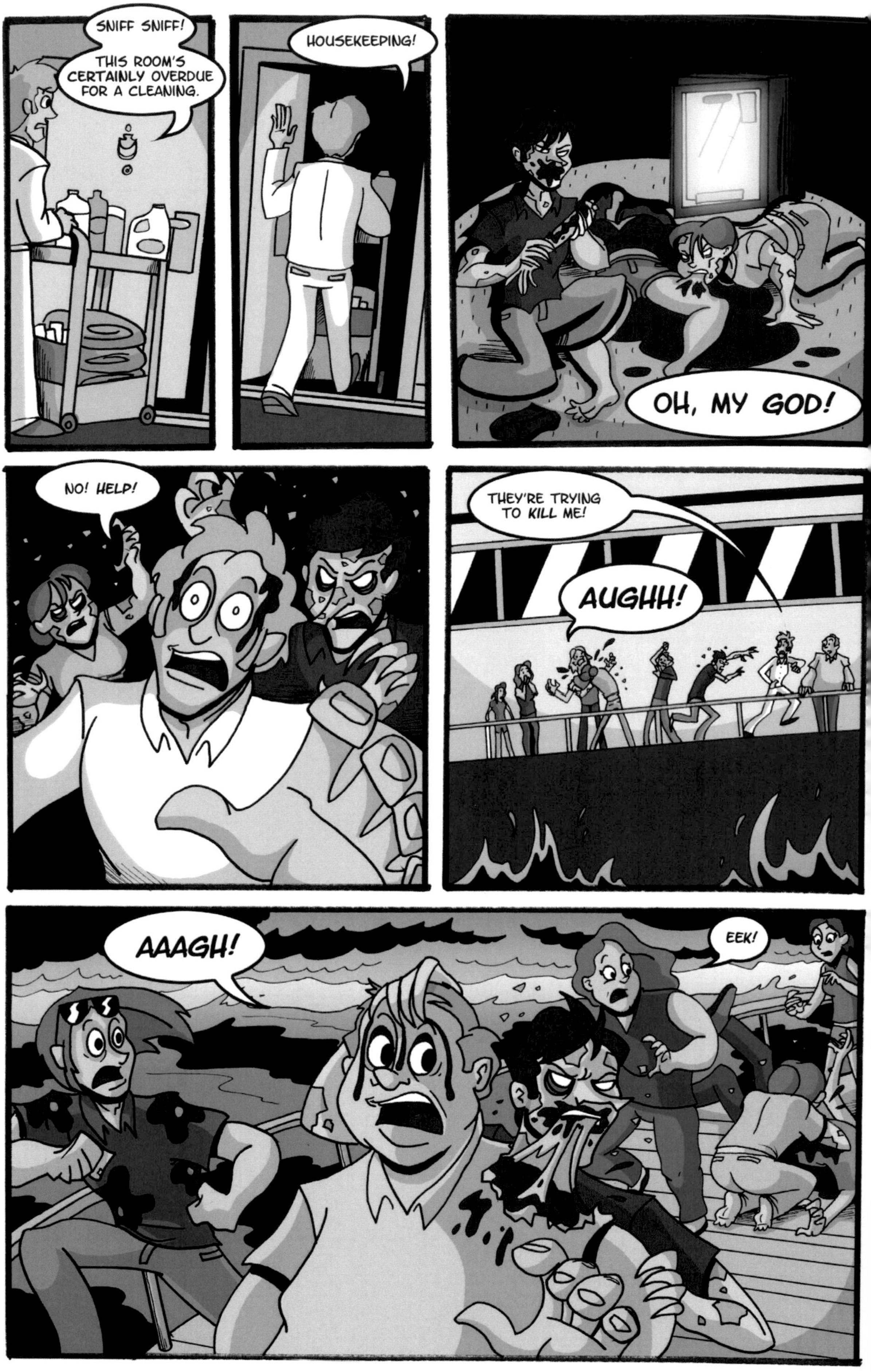
SNIFF SNIFF!
THIS ROOM'S CERTAINLY OVERDUE FOR A CLEANING.
HOUSEKEEPING!
OH, MY GOD!
NO! HELP!
THEY'RE TRYING TO KILL ME!
AUGHH!
AAAGH!
EEK!

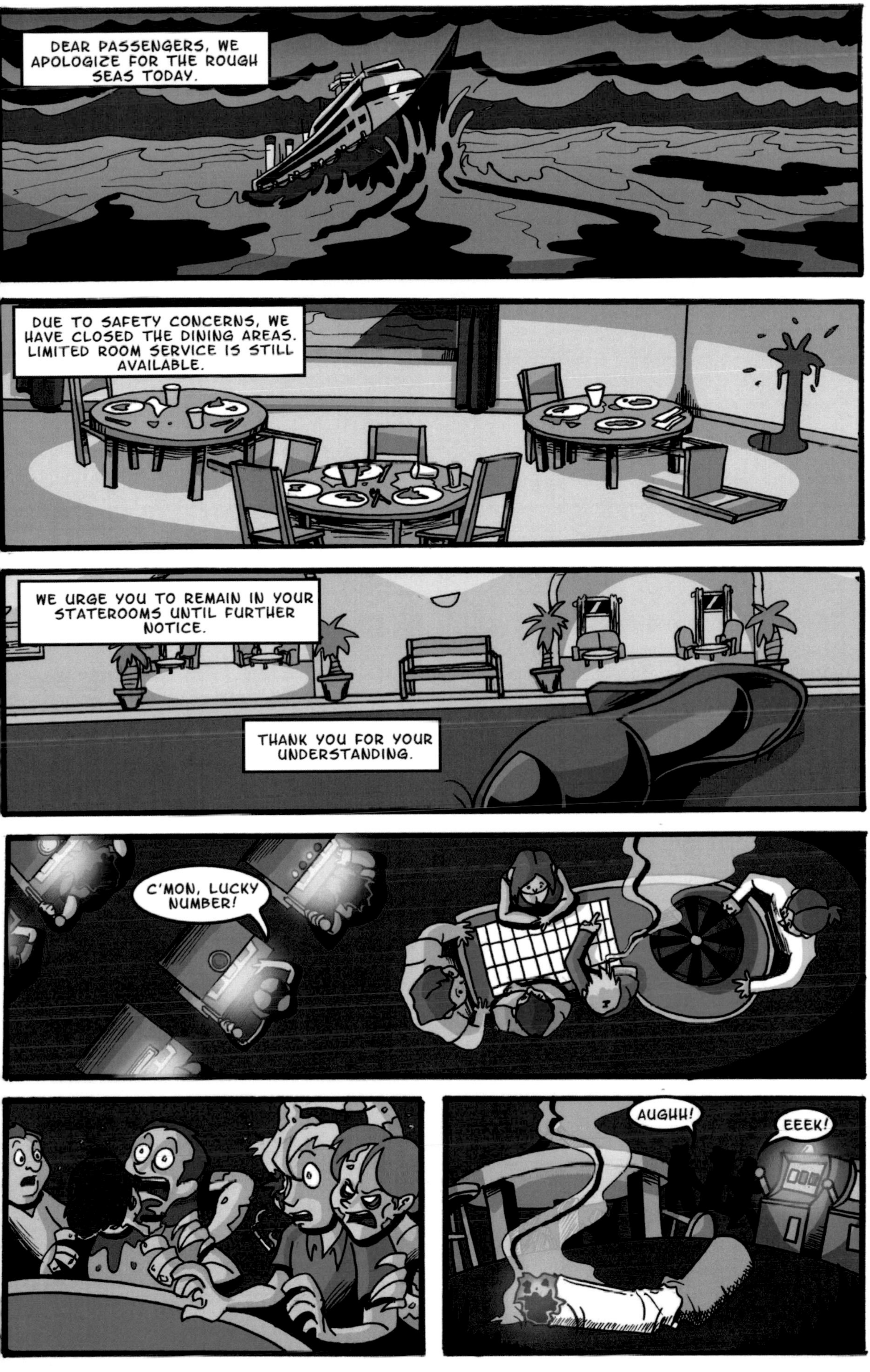
DEAR PASSENGERS, WE APOLOGIZE FOR THE ROUGH SEAS TODAY.
DUE TO SAFETY CONCERNS, WE HAVE CLOSED THE DINING AREAS. LIMITED ROOM SERVICE IS STILL AVAILABLE.
WE URGE YOU TO REMAIN IN YOUR STATEROOMS UNTIL FURTHER NOTICE.
THANK YOU FOR YOUR UNDERSTANDING.
C'MON, LUCKY NUMBER!
AUGHH!
EEEK!

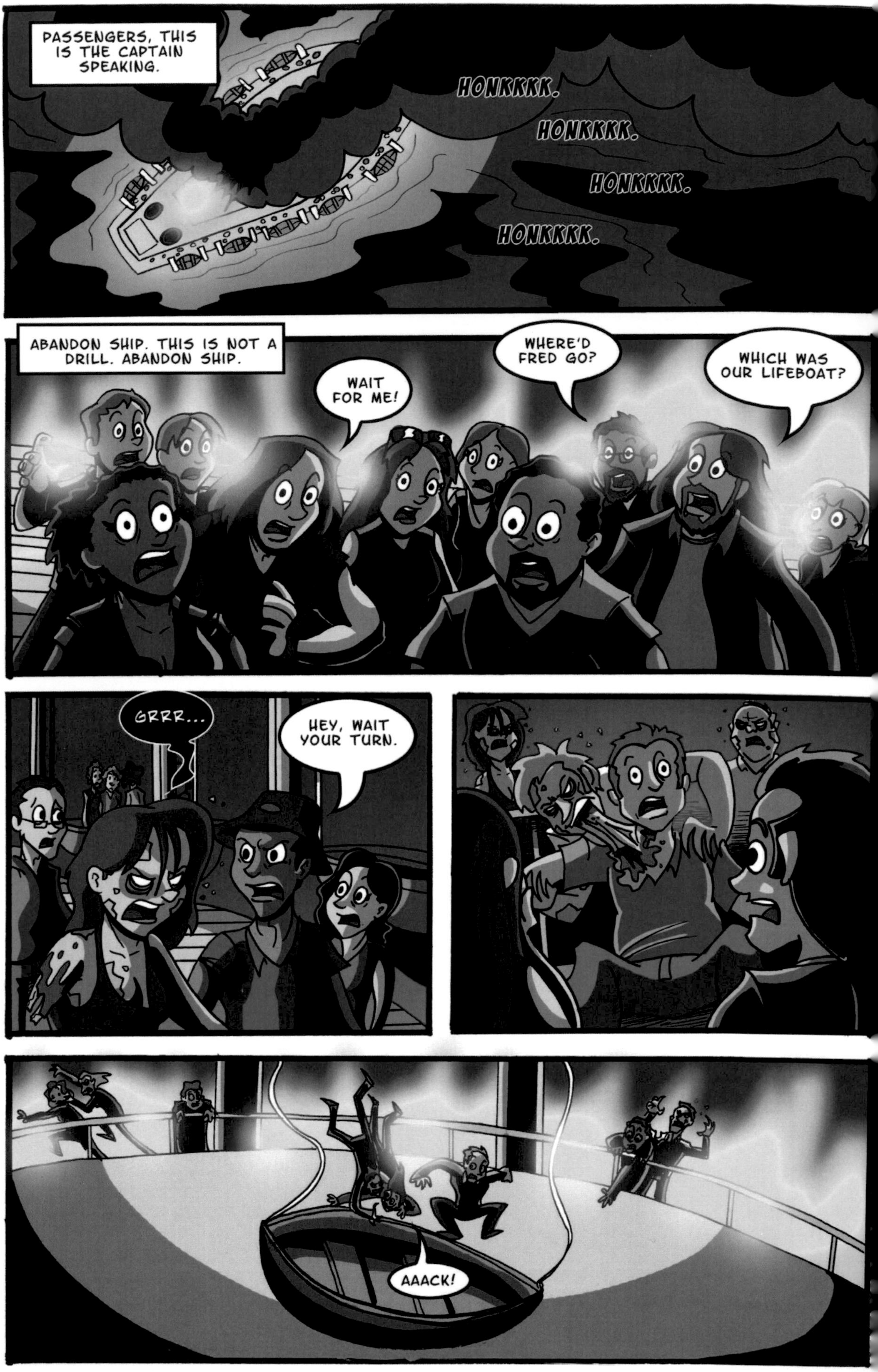
PASSENGERS, THIS IS THE CAPTAIN SPEAKING.
HONKKKK.
HONKKKK.
HONKKKK.
HONKKKK.
ABANDON SHIP. THIS IS NOT A DRILL. ABANDON SHIP.
WAIT FOR ME!
WHERE'D FRED GO?
WHICH WAS OUR LIFEBOAT?
GRRR...
HEY, WAIT YOUR TURN.
AAACK!

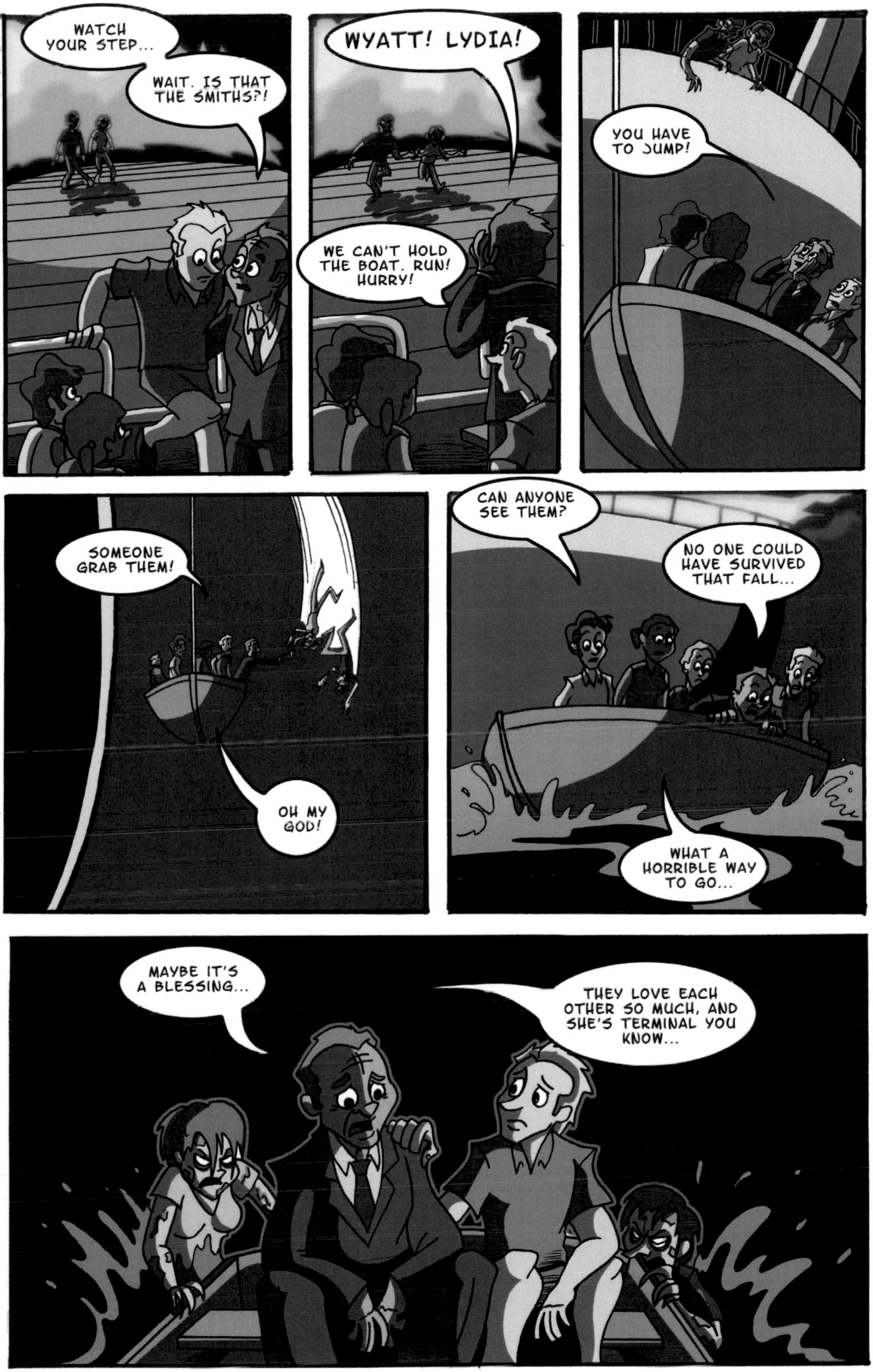
WATCH YOUR STEP...
WAIT. IS THAT THE SMITHS?!
WYATT! LYDIA!
WE CAN'T HOLD THE BOAT. RUN! HURRY!
YOU HAVE TO JUMP!
SOMEONE GRAB THEM!
OH MY GOD!
CAN ANYONE SEE THEM?
NO ONE COULD HAVE SURVIVED THAT FALL...
WHAT A HORRIBLE WAY TO GO...
MAYBE IT'S A BLESSING...
THEY LOVE EACH OTHER SO MUCH, AND SHE'S TERMINAL YOU KNOW...

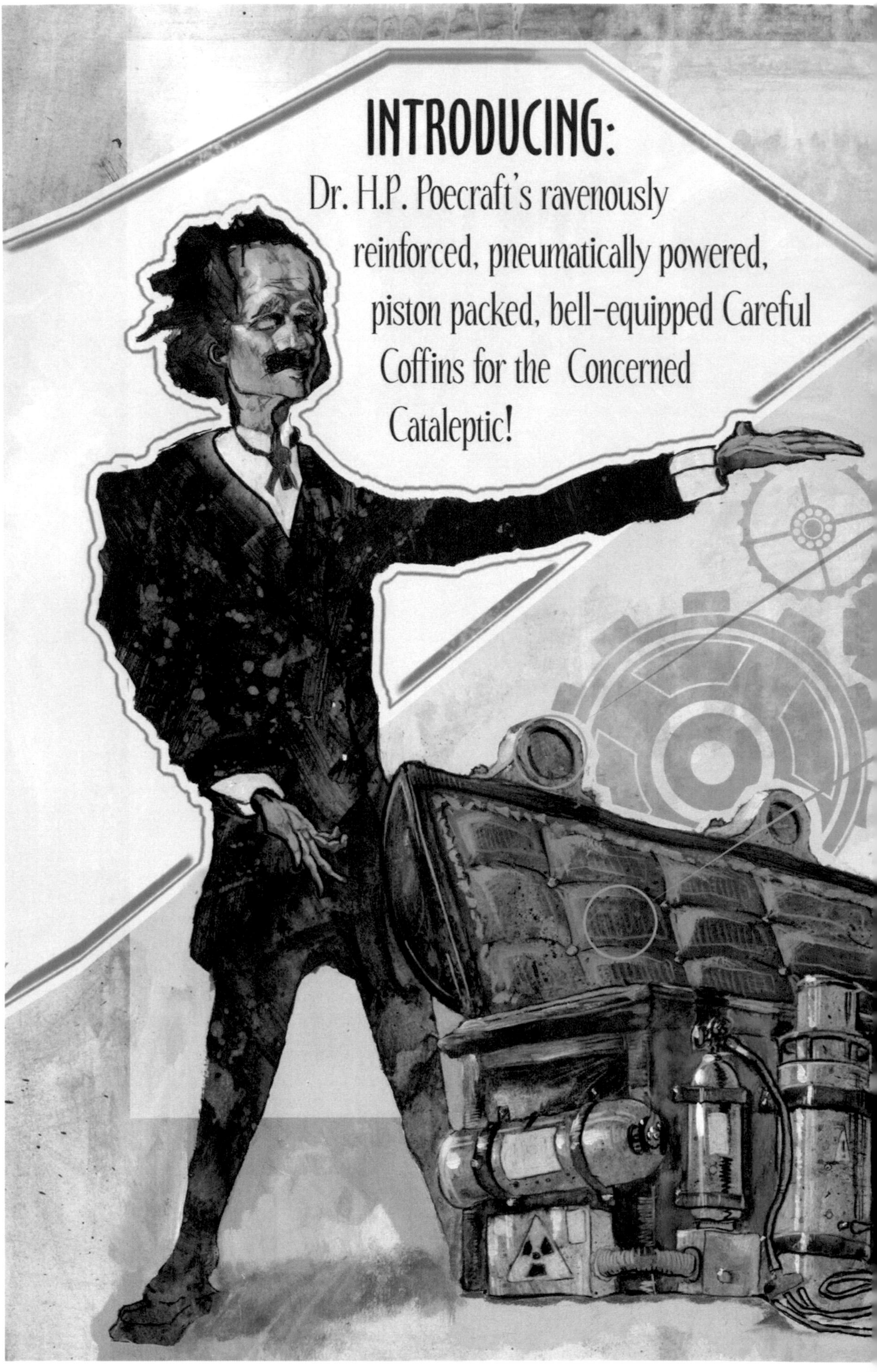
INTRODUCING:
Dr. H.P. Poecraft's ravenously reinforced, pneumatically powered, piston packed, bell-equipped Careful Coffins for the Concerned Cataleptic!

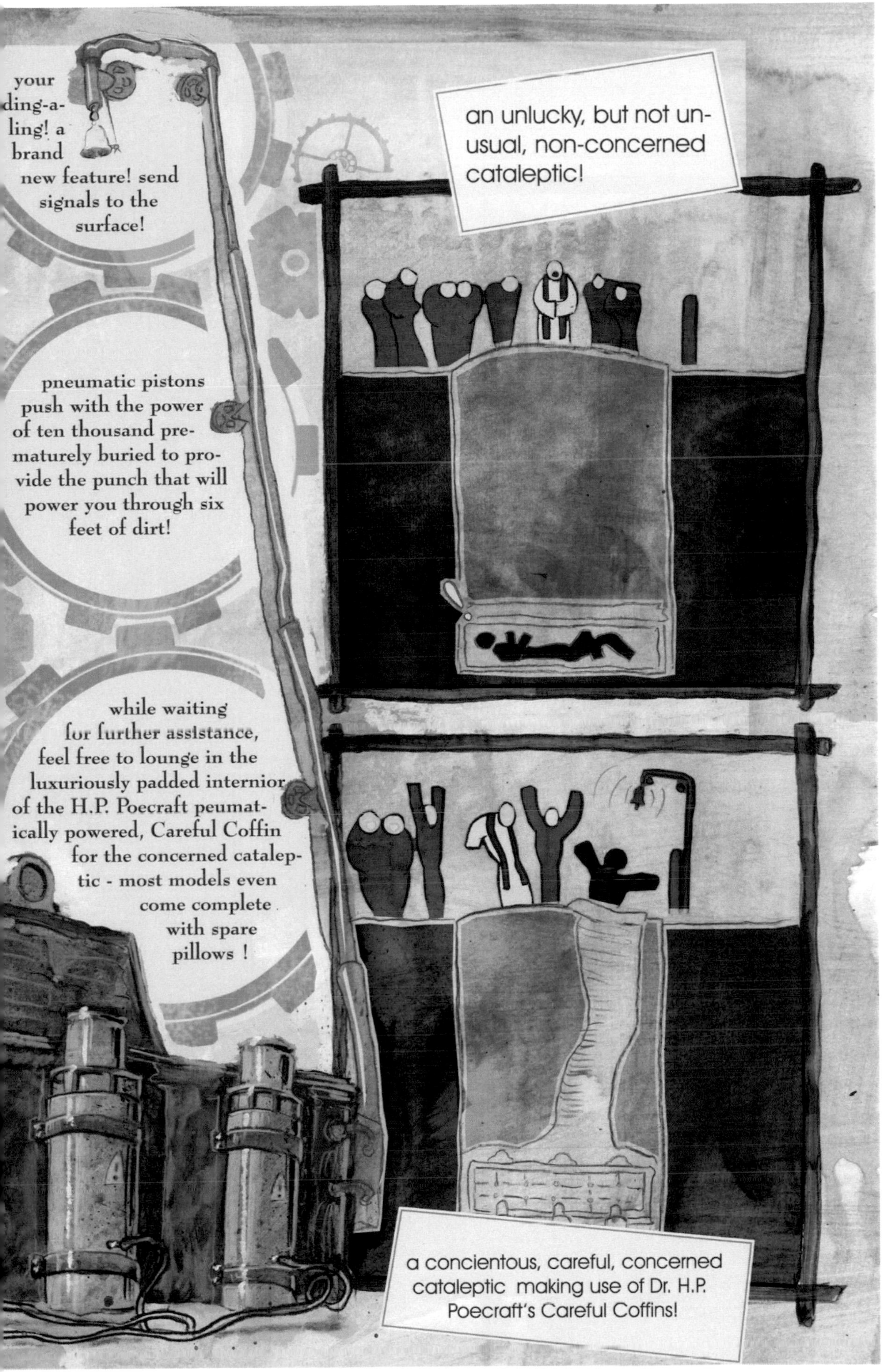
your ding-a-ling! a brand new feature! send signals to the surface!
an unlucky, but not un-usual, non-concerned cataleptic!
pneumatic pistons push with the power of ten thousand pre-maturely buried to pro-vide the punch that will power you through six feet of dirt!
while waiting for further assistance, feel free to lounge in the luxuriously padded internior of the H.P. Poecraft peumat-ically powered, Careful Coffin for the concerned catalep-tic - most models even come complete with spare pillows !
a concientous, careful, concerned cataleptic making use of Dr. H.P. Poecraft's Careful Coffins!

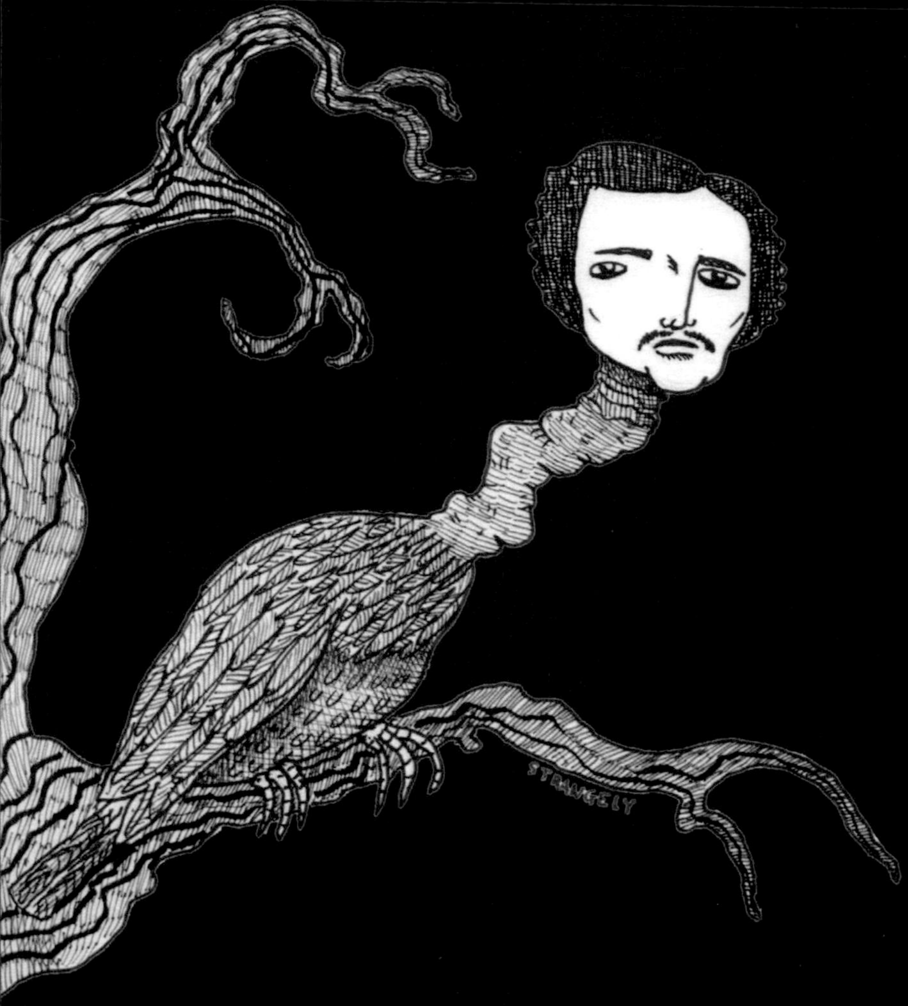
STRANGELY

HE HAD COME LIKE A THIEF IN THE NIGHT. AND ONE BY ONE DROPPED THE REVELLERS IN THE BLOOD-BEDEWED HALLS OF THEIR REVEL, AND DIED EACH IN THE DESPAIRING POSTURE OF HIS FALL.

from "THE MASQUE OF THE RED DEATH"

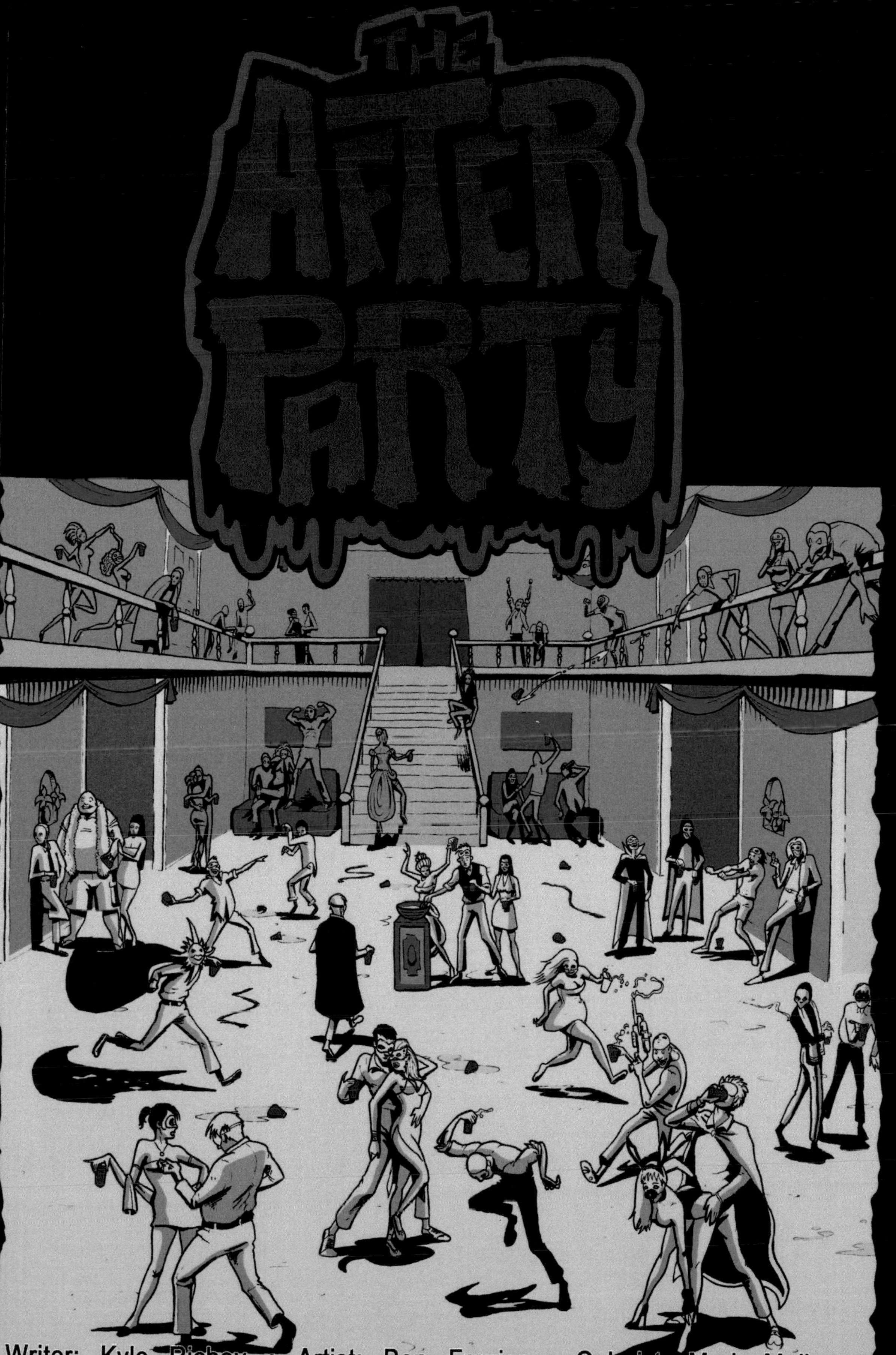
THE AFTER PARTY

Writer: Kyle Richey • Artist: Ben Frazier • Colorist: Mark Mullaney

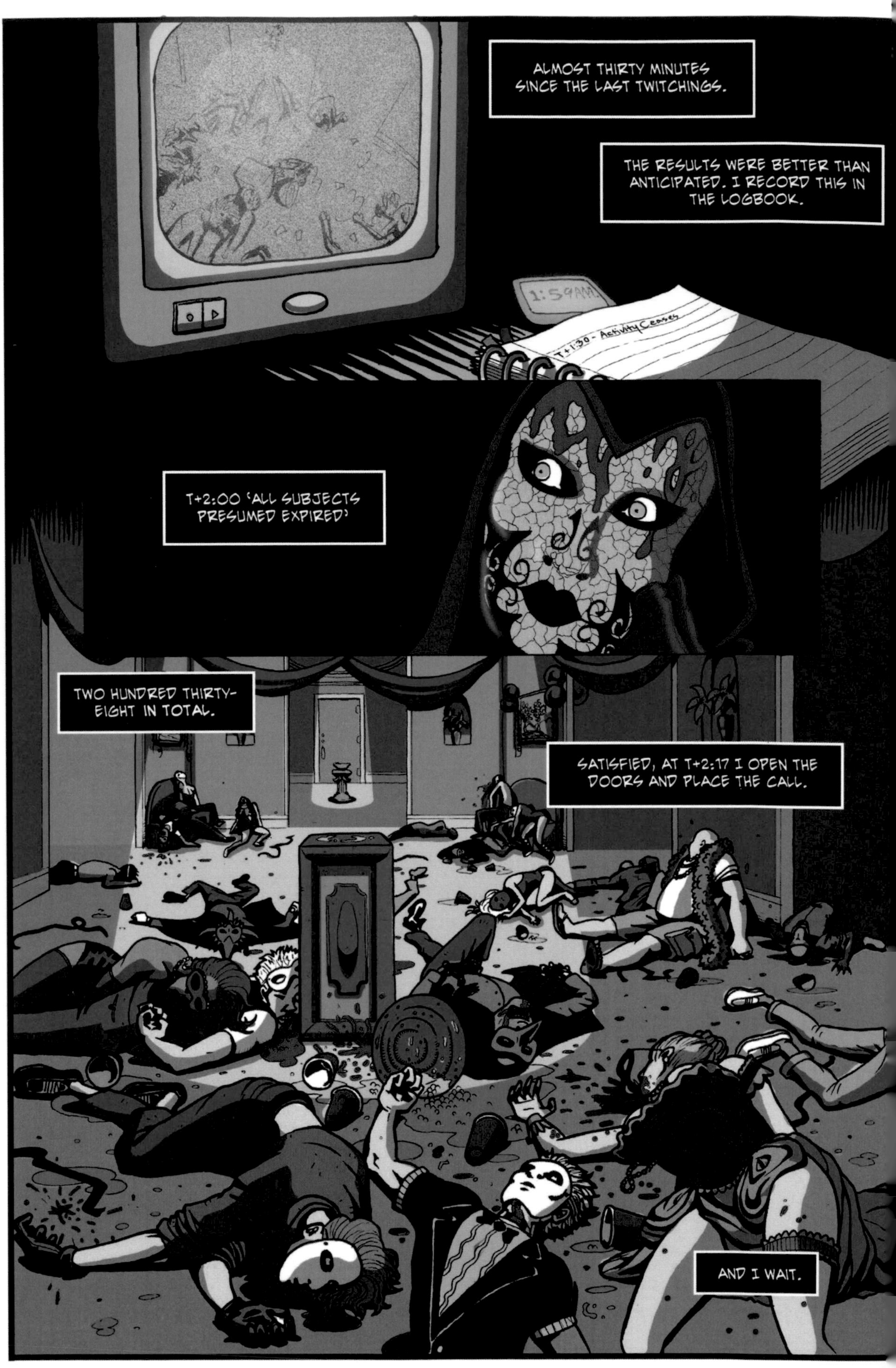
ALMOST THIRTY MINUTES SINCE THE LAST TWITCHINGS.
THE RESULTS WERE BETTER THAN ANTICIPATED. I RECORD THIS IN THE LOGBOOK.
1:59AM
T+1:30 - Activity Ceases
T+2:00 'ALL SUBJECTS PRESUMED EXPIRED'
TWO HUNDRED THIRTY-EIGHT IN TOTAL.
SATISFIED, AT T+2:17 I OPEN THE DOORS AND PLACE THE CALL.
AND I WAIT.

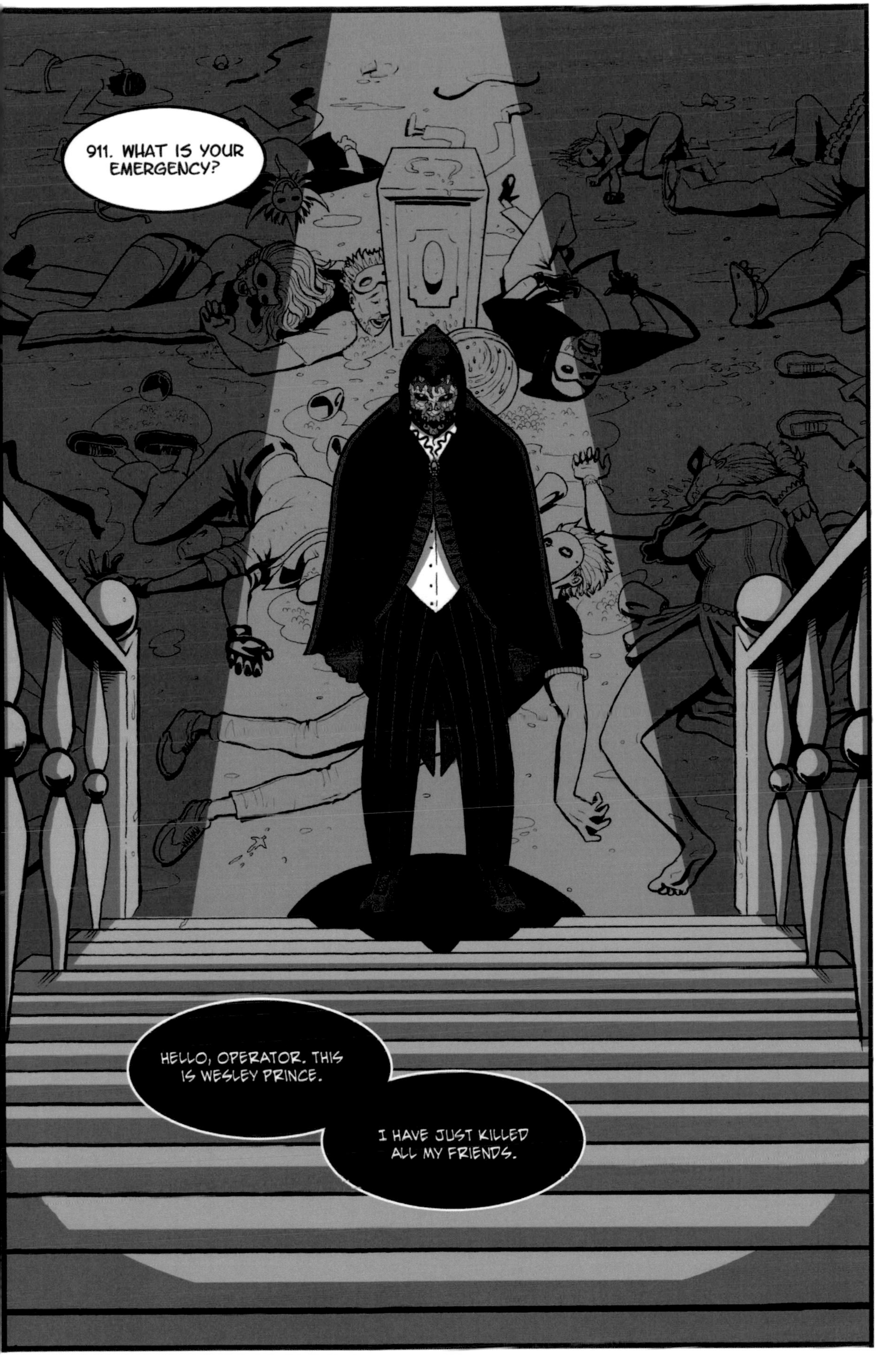
911. WHAT IS YOUR EMERGENCY?
HELLO, OPERATOR. THIS IS WESLEY PRINCE.
I HAVE JUST KILLED ALL MY FRIENDS.

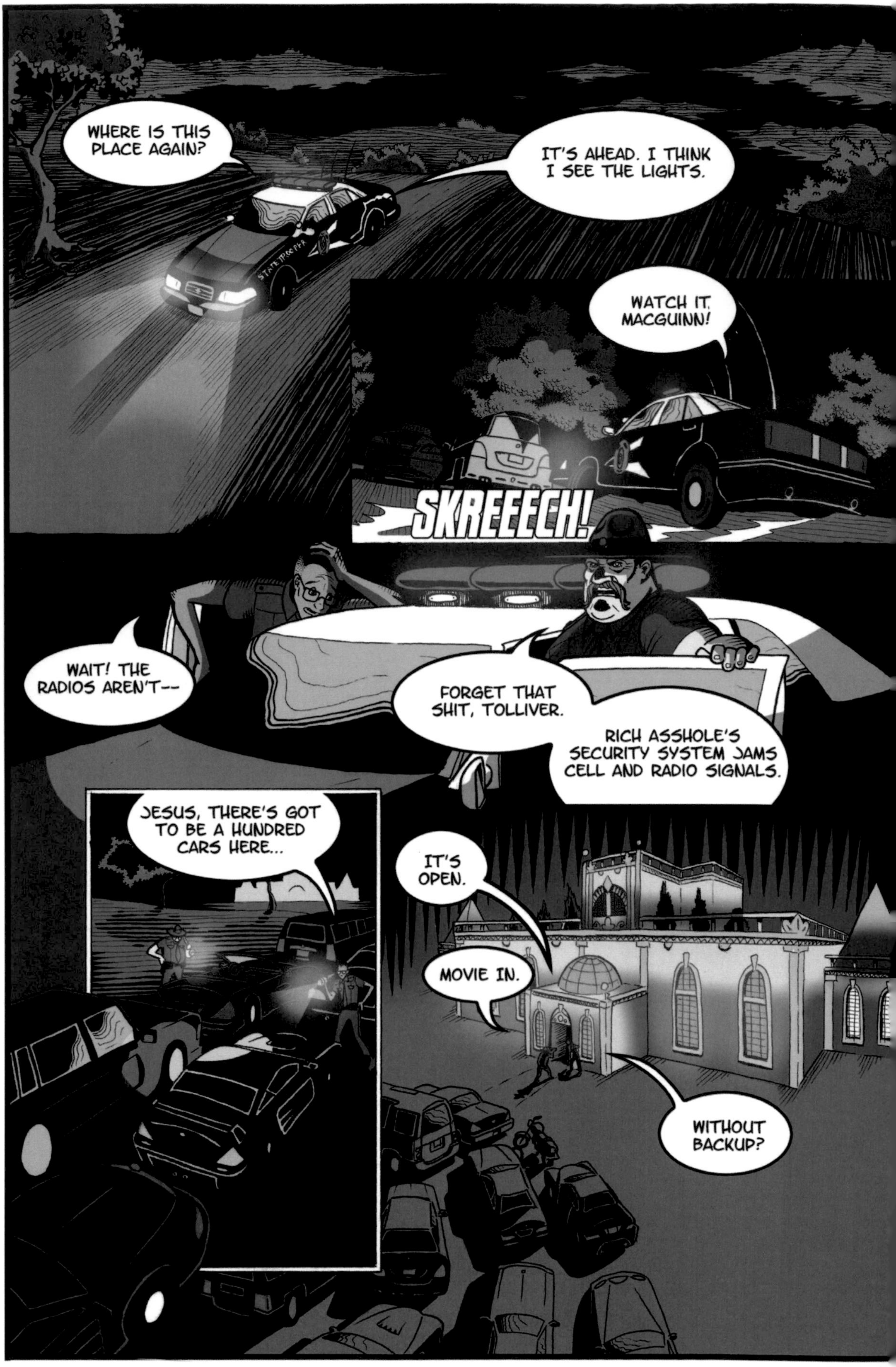
WHERE IS THIS PLACE AGAIN?
IT'S AHEAD. I THINK I SEE THE LIGHTS.
STATE TROOPER
WATCH IT, MACGUINN!
SKREEECH!
WAIT! THE RADIOS AREN'T--
FORGET THAT SHIT, TOLLIVER.
RICH ASSHOLE'S SECURITY SYSTEM JAMS CELL AND RADIO SIGNALS.
JESUS, THERE'S GOT TO BE A HUNDRED CARS HERE...
IT'S OPEN.
MOVIE IN.
WITHOUT BACKUP?

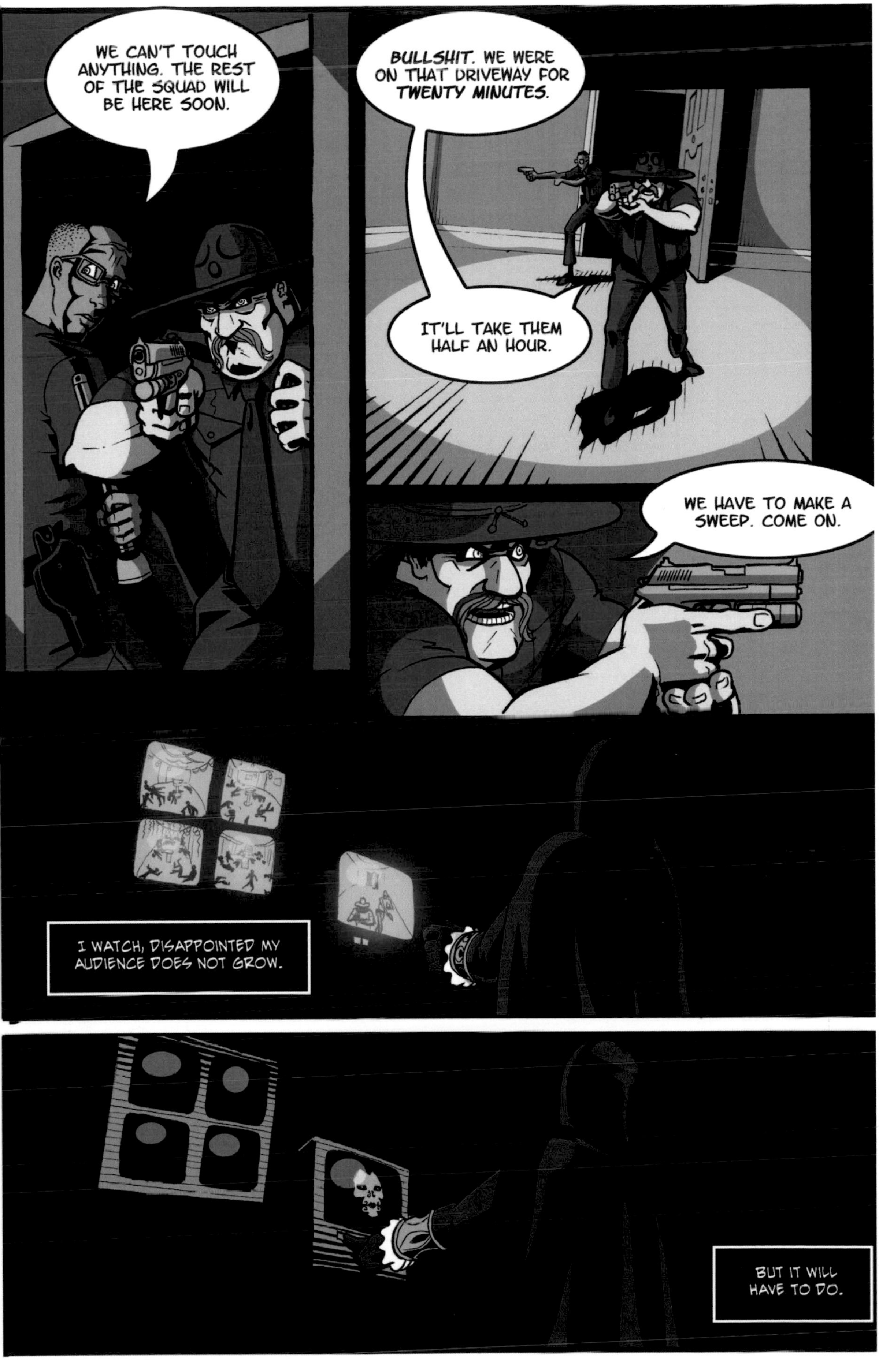
WE CAN'T TOUCH ANYTHING. THE REST OF THE SQUAD WILL BE HERE SOON.
BULLSHIT. WE WERE ON THAT DRIVEWAY FOR TWENTY MINUTES.
IT'LL TAKE THEM HALF AN HOUR.
WE HAVE TO MAKE A SWEEP. COME ON.
I WATCH, DISAPPOINTED MY AUDIENCE DOES NOT GROW.
BUT IT WILL HAVE TO DO.

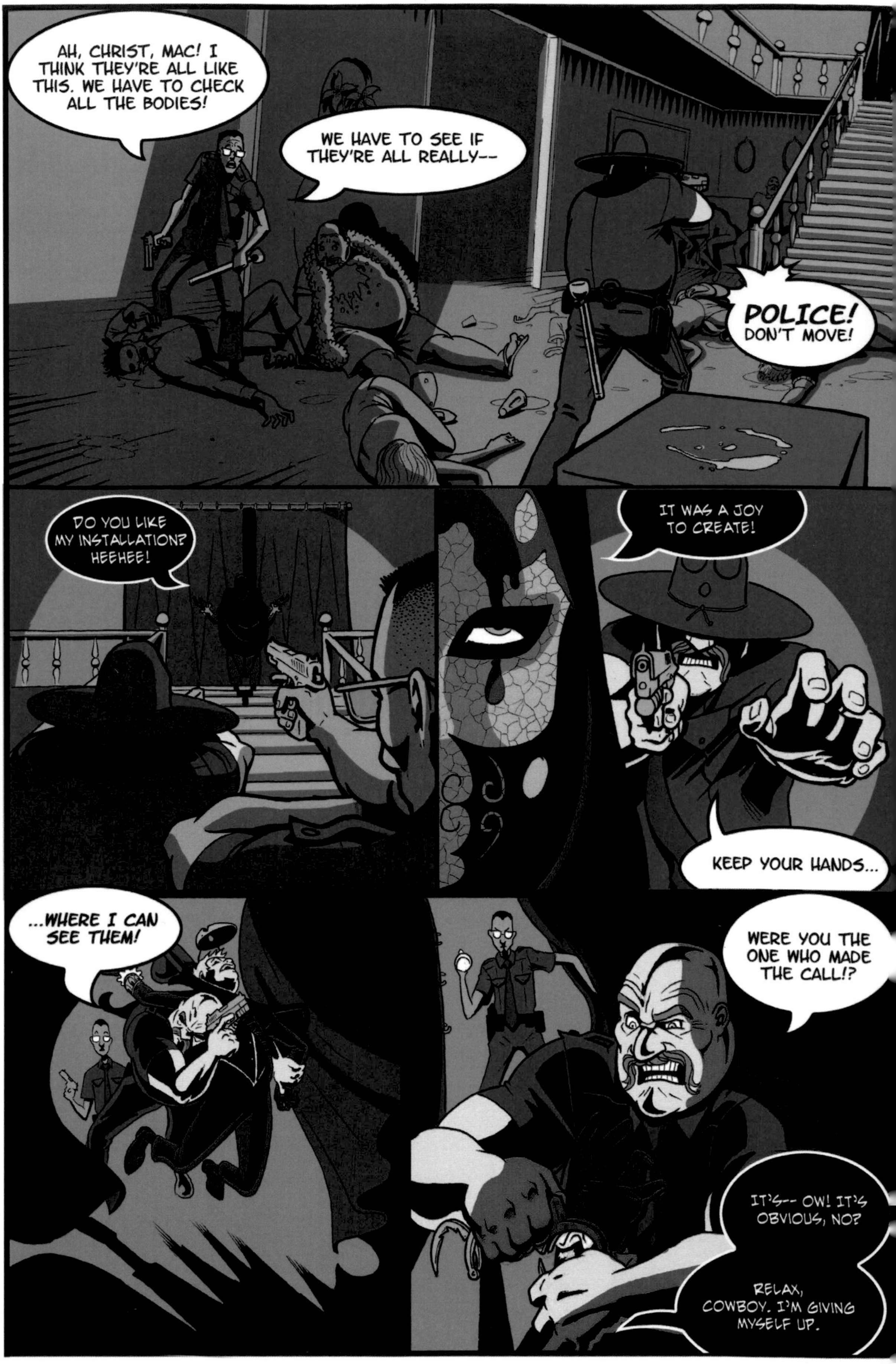
AH, CHRIST, MAC! I THINK THEY'RE ALL LIKE THIS. WE HAVE TO CHECK ALL THE BODIES!
WE HAVE TO SEE IF THEY'RE ALL REALLY--
POLICE! DON'T MOVE!
DO YOU LIKE MY INSTALLATION? HEEHEE!
IT WAS A JOY TO CREATE!
KEEP YOUR HANDS...
...WHERE I CAN SEE THEM!
WERE YOU THE ONE WHO MADE THE CALL!?
IT'S-- OW! IT'S OBVIOUS, NO?
RELAX, COWBOY. I'M GIVING MYSELF UP.

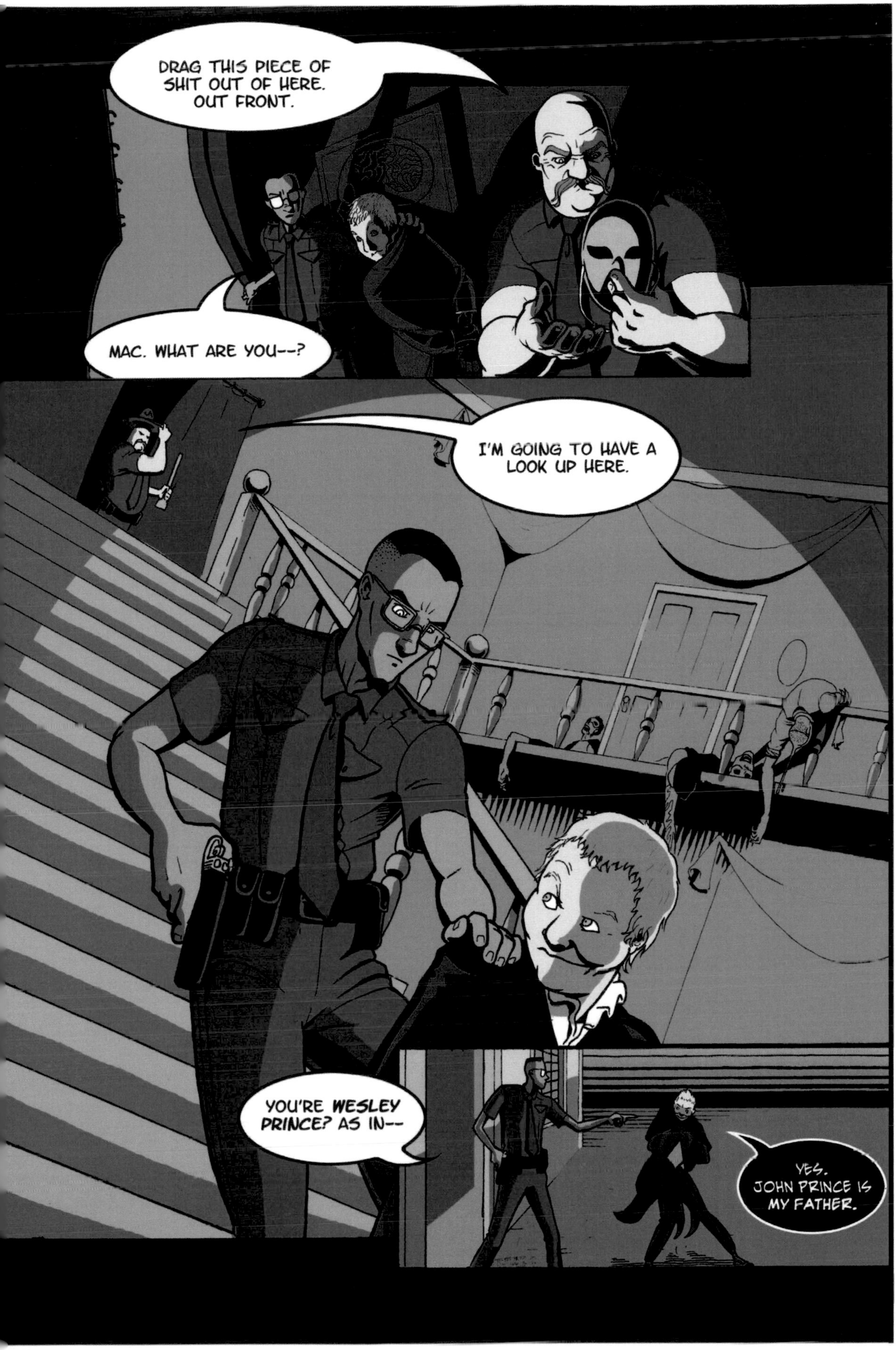
DRAG THIS PIECE OF SHIT OUT OF HERE. OUT FRONT.
MAC. WHAT ARE YOU--?
I'M GOING TO HAVE A LOOK UP HERE.
YOU'RE WESLEY PRINCE? AS IN--
YES. JOHN PRINCE IS MY FATHER.

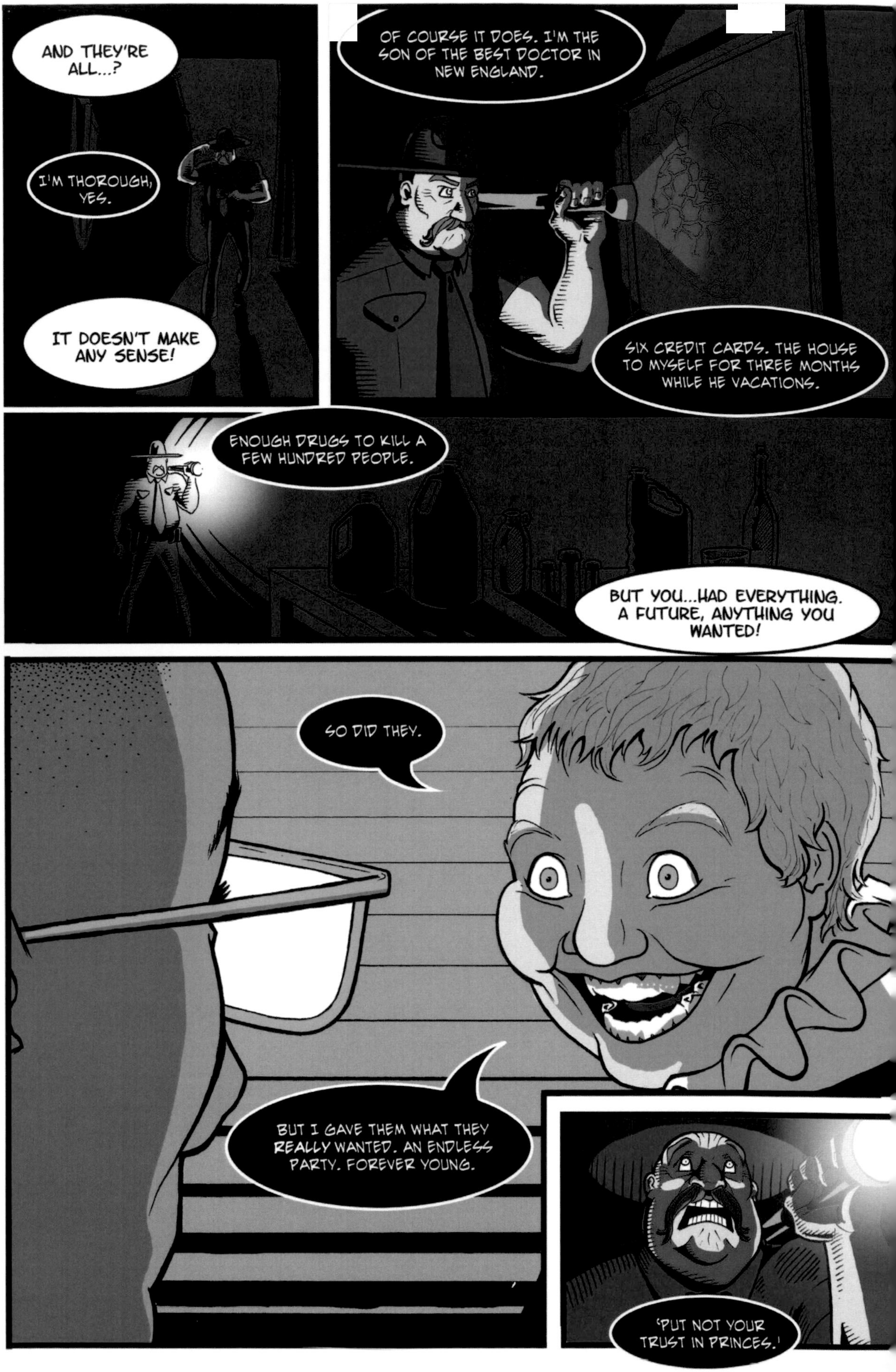
AND THEY'RE ALL...?
I'M THOROUGH, YES.
IT DOESN'T MAKE ANY SENSE!
OF COURSE IT DOES. I'M THE SON OF THE BEST DOCTOR IN NEW ENGLAND.
SIX CREDIT CARDS. THE HOUSE TO MYSELF FOR THREE MONTHS WHILE HE VACATIONS.
ENOUGH DRUGS TO KILL A FEW HUNDRED PEOPLE.
BUT YOU...HAD EVERYTHING. A FUTURE, ANYTHING YOU WANTED!
SO DID THEY.
BUT I GAVE THEM WHAT THEY REALLY WANTED. AN ENDLESS PARTY. FOREVER YOUNG.
'PUT NOT YOUR TRUST IN PRINCES.'

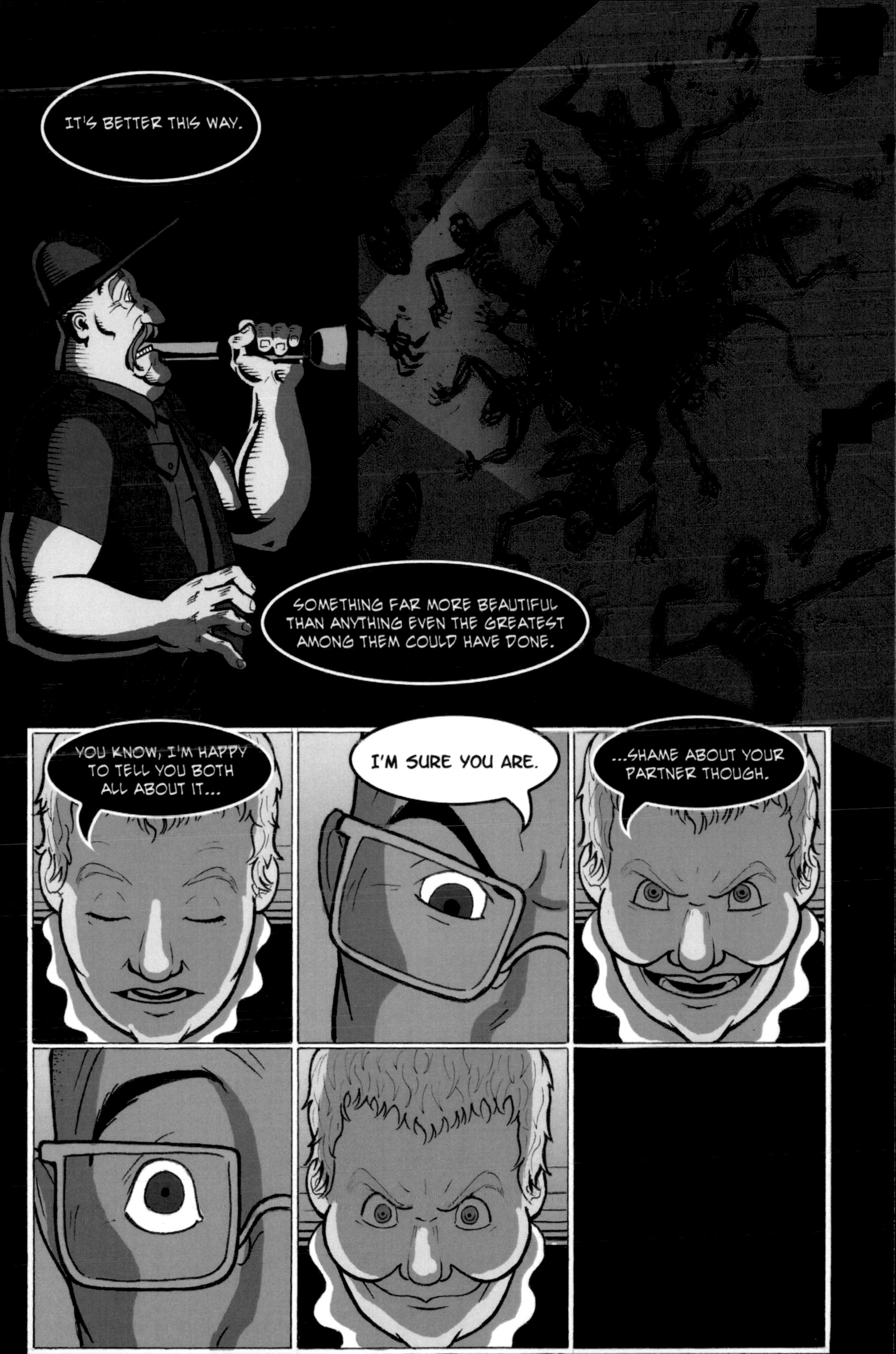
IT'S BETTER THIS WAY.
SOMETHING FAR MORE BEAUTIFUL THAN ANYTHING EVEN THE GREATEST AMONG THEM COULD HAVE DONE.
YOU KNOW, I'M HAPPY TO TELL YOU BOTH ALL ABOUT IT...
I'M SURE YOU ARE.
...SHAME ABOUT YOUR PARTNER THOUGH.

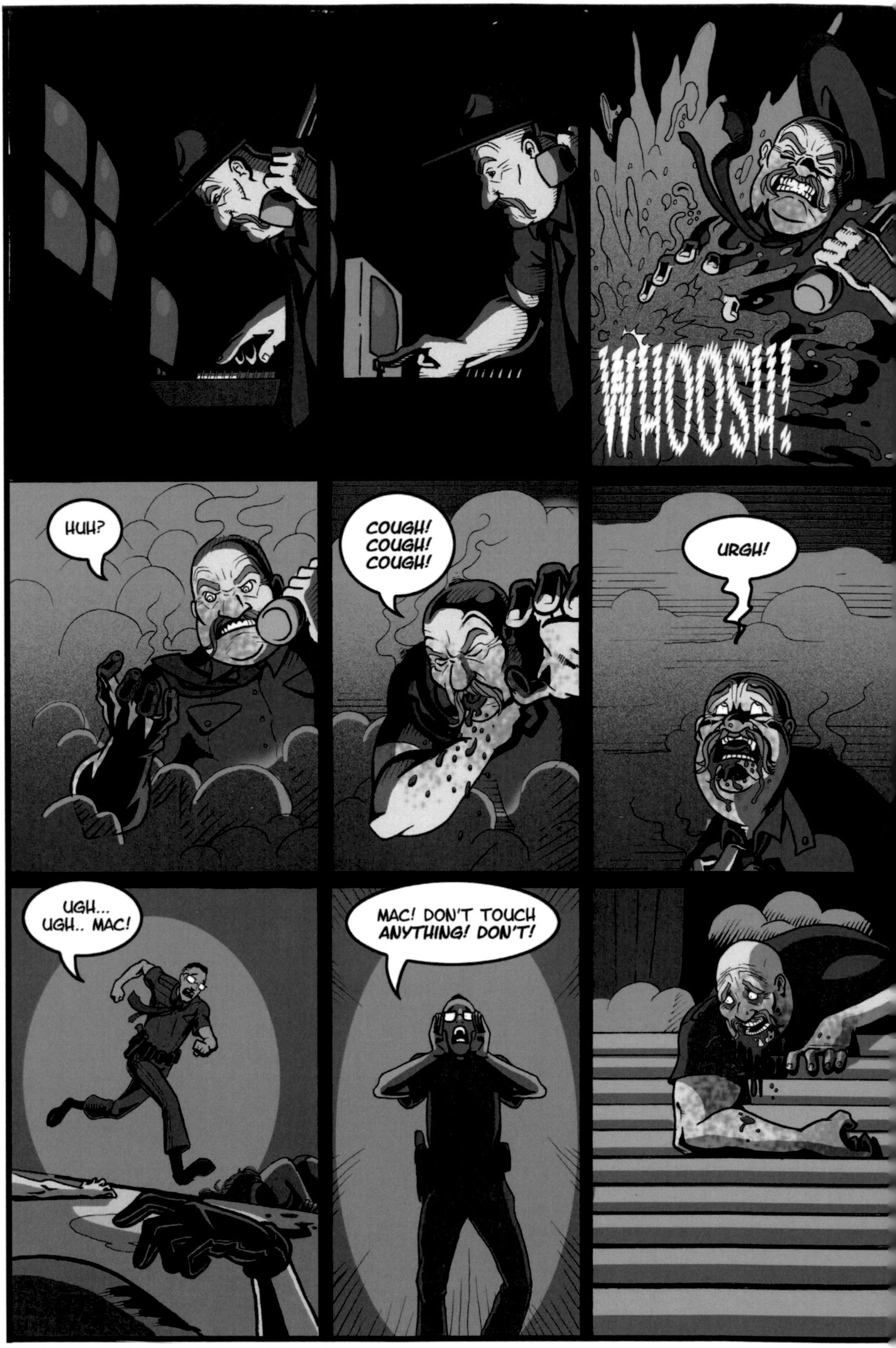
WHOOSH!
HUH?
COUGH!
COUGH!
COUGH!
URGH!
UGH...
UGH.. MAC!
MAC! DON'T TOUCH
ANYTHING! DON'T!

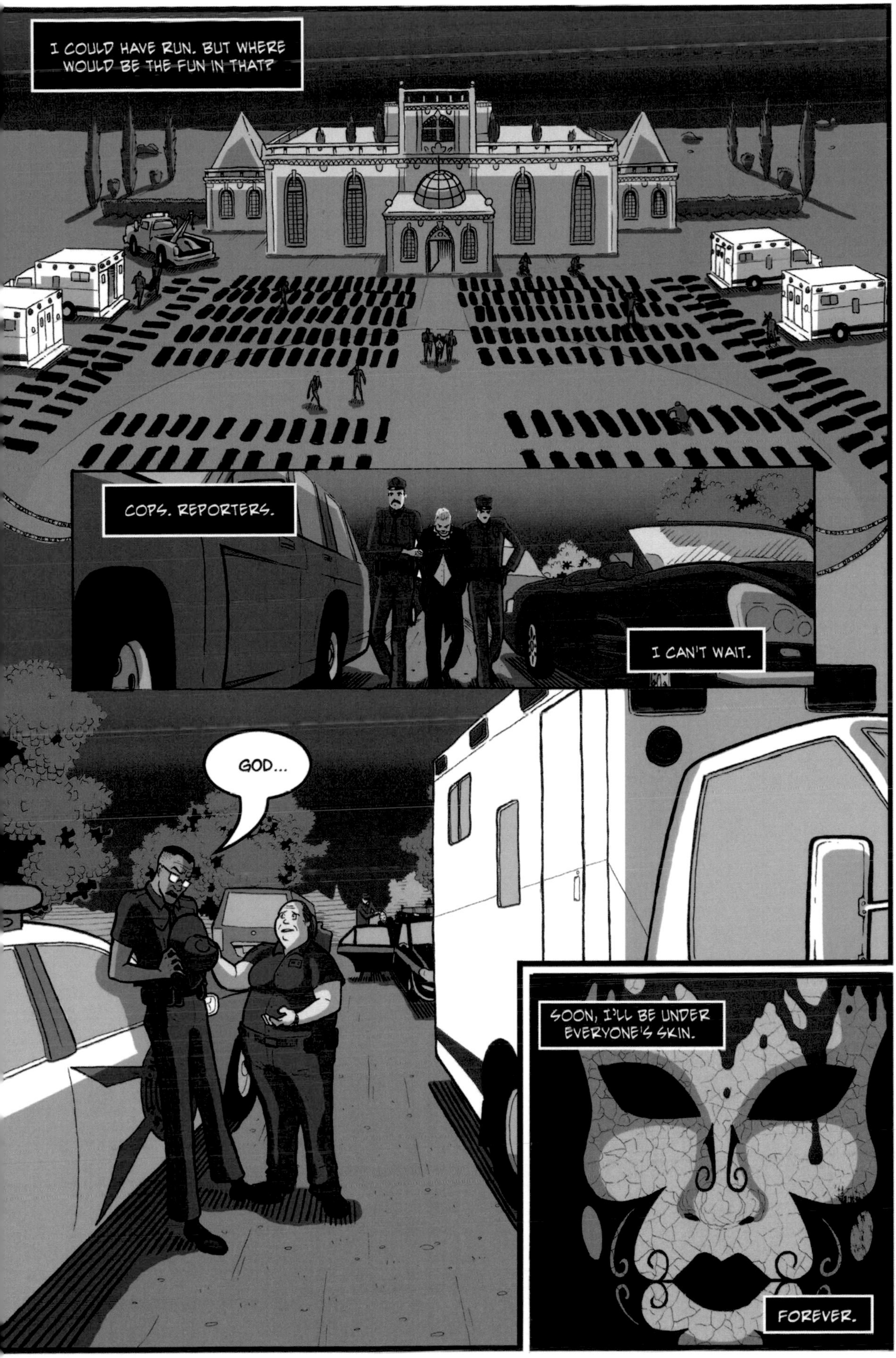
I COULD HAVE RUN. BUT WHERE WOULD BE THE FUN IN THAT?
COPS. REPORTERS.
I CAN'T WAIT.
GOD...
SOON, I'LL BE UNDER EVERYONE'S SKIN.
FOREVER.

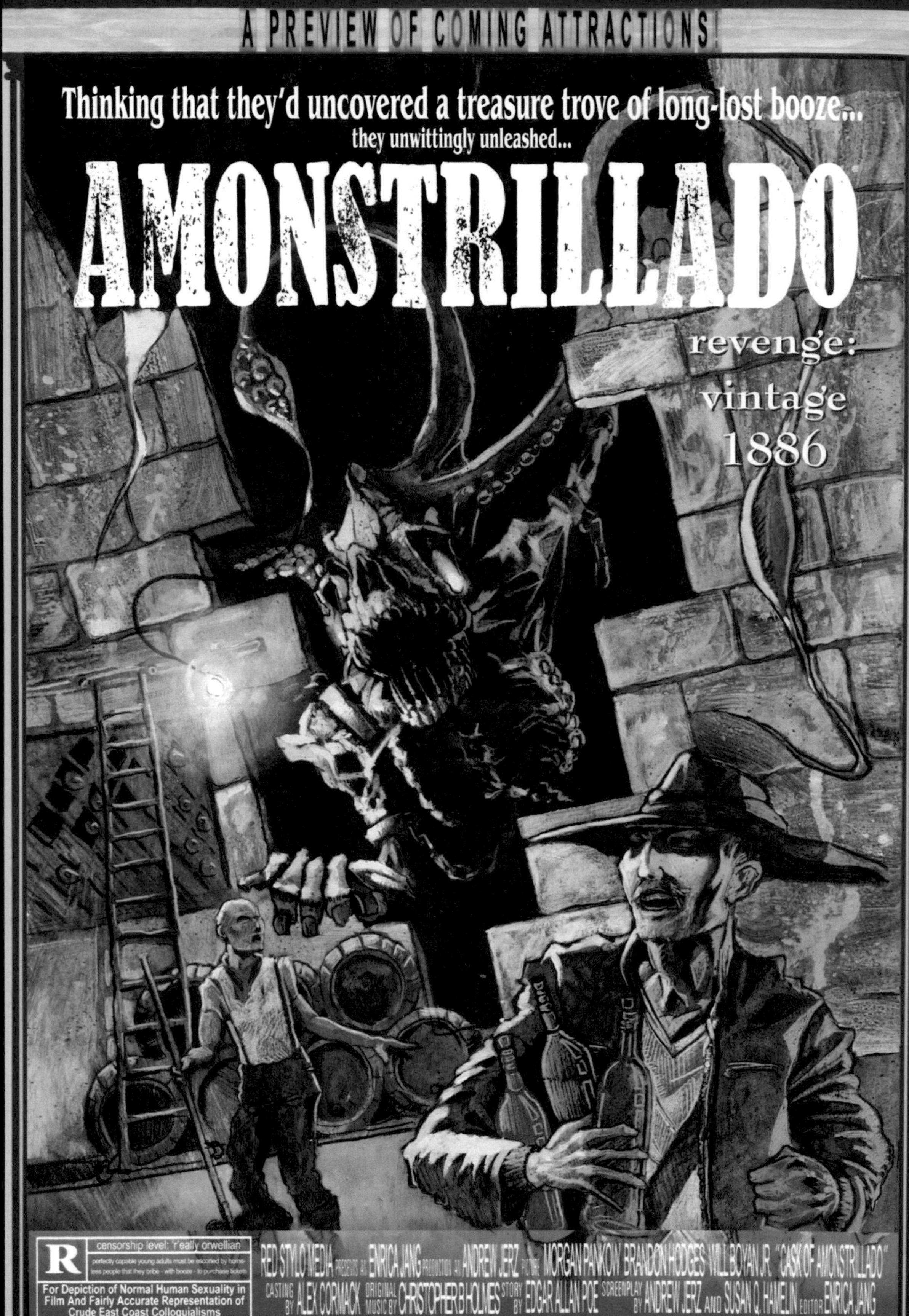
A PREVIEW OF COMING ATTRACTIONS!
Thinking that they'd uncovered a treasure trove of long-lost booze...
they unwittingly unleashed...
AMONSTRILLADO
revenge: vintage 1886
R
censorship level: 'r'eally orwellian
perfectly capable young adults must be escorted by homeless people that they bribe - with booze - to purchase tickets
For Depiction of Normal Human Sexuality in Film And Fairly Accurate Representation of Crude East Coast Colloquialisms
RED STYLO MEDIA PRESENTS AN ENRICA JANG PRODUCTION AN ANDREW JERZ MORGAN PANKOW BRANDON HODGES WILL BOYAN JR. "CASK OF AMONSTRILLADO"
CASTING BY ALEX CORMACK ORIGINAL MUSIC BY CHRISTOPHER B HOLMES STORY BY EDGAR ALLAN POE SCREENPLAY BY ANDREW JERZ AND SUSAN Q. HAMELIN EDITOR ENRICA JANG

MY IMMEDIATE PURPOSE IS TO PLACE BEFORE THE WORLD, PLAINLY, SUCCINCTLY, AND WITHOUT COMMENT, A SERIES OF MERE HOUSEHOLD EVENTS.

from "THE BLACK CAT"

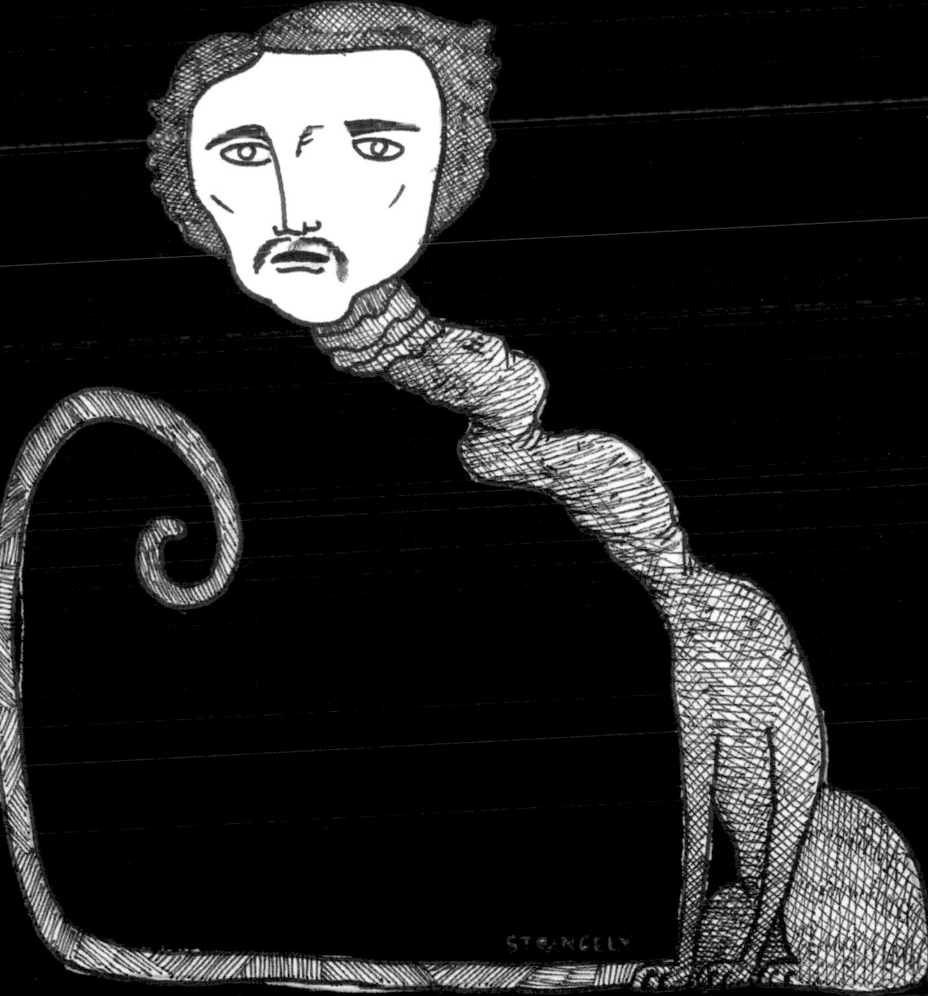

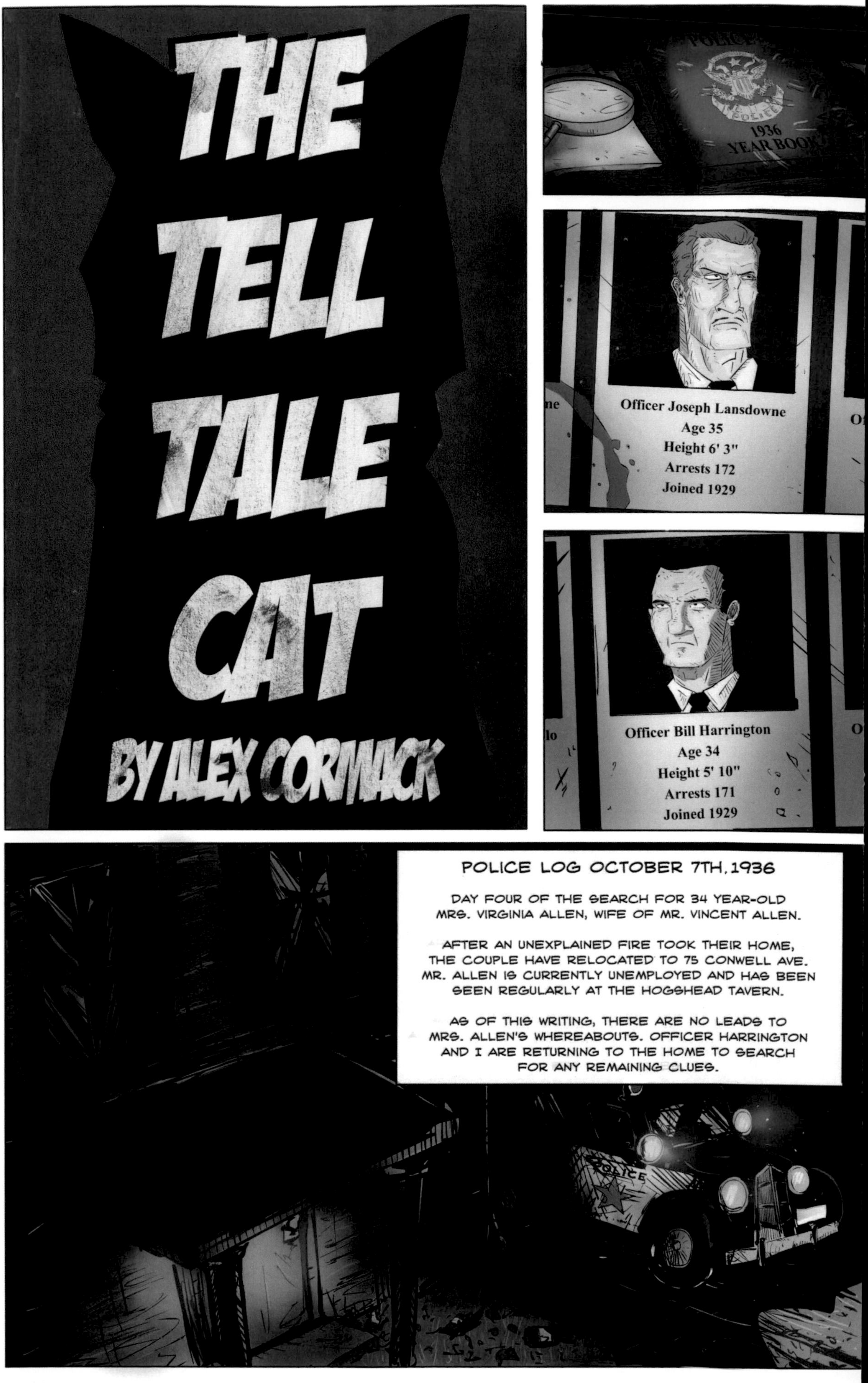
THE TELL TALE CAT
BY ALEX CORMACK
POLICE
1936
YEAR BOOK
Officer Joseph Lansdowne
Age 35
Height 6' 3"
Arrests 172
Joined 1929
Officer Bill Harrington
Age 34
Height 5' 10"
Arrests 171
Joined 1929
POLICE LOG OCTOBER 7TH, 1936
DAY FOUR OF THE SEARCH FOR 34 YEAR-OLD MRS. VIRGINIA ALLEN, WIFE OF MR. VINCENT ALLEN.
AFTER AN UNEXPLAINED FIRE TOOK THEIR HOME, THE COUPLE HAVE RELOCATED TO 75 CONWELL AVE. MR. ALLEN IS CURRENTLY UNEMPLOYED AND HAS BEEN SEEN REGULARLY AT THE HOGSHEAD TAVERN.
AS OF THIS WRITING, THERE ARE NO LEADS TO MRS. ALLEN'S WHEREABOUTS. OFFICER HARRINGTON AND I ARE RETURNING TO THE HOME TO SEARCH FOR ANY REMAINING CLUES.
POLICE

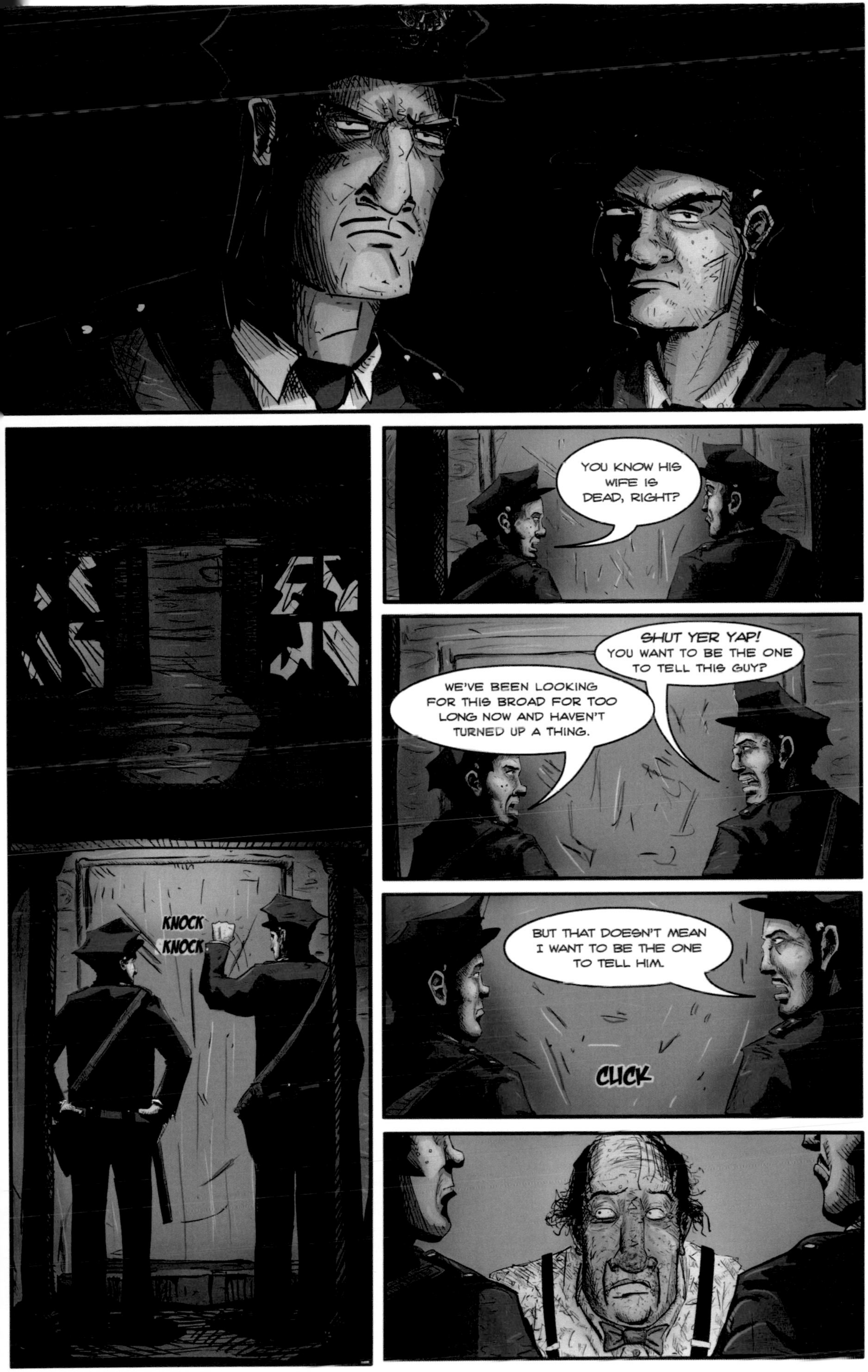

YOU KNOW HIS WIFE IS DEAD, RIGHT?
SHUT YER YAP! YOU WANT TO BE THE ONE TO TELL THIS GUY?
WE'VE BEEN LOOKING FOR THIS BROAD FOR TOO LONG NOW AND HAVEN'T TURNED UP A THING.
KNOCK KNOCK
BUT THAT DOESN'T MEAN I WANT TO BE THE ONE TO TELL HIM.
CLICK

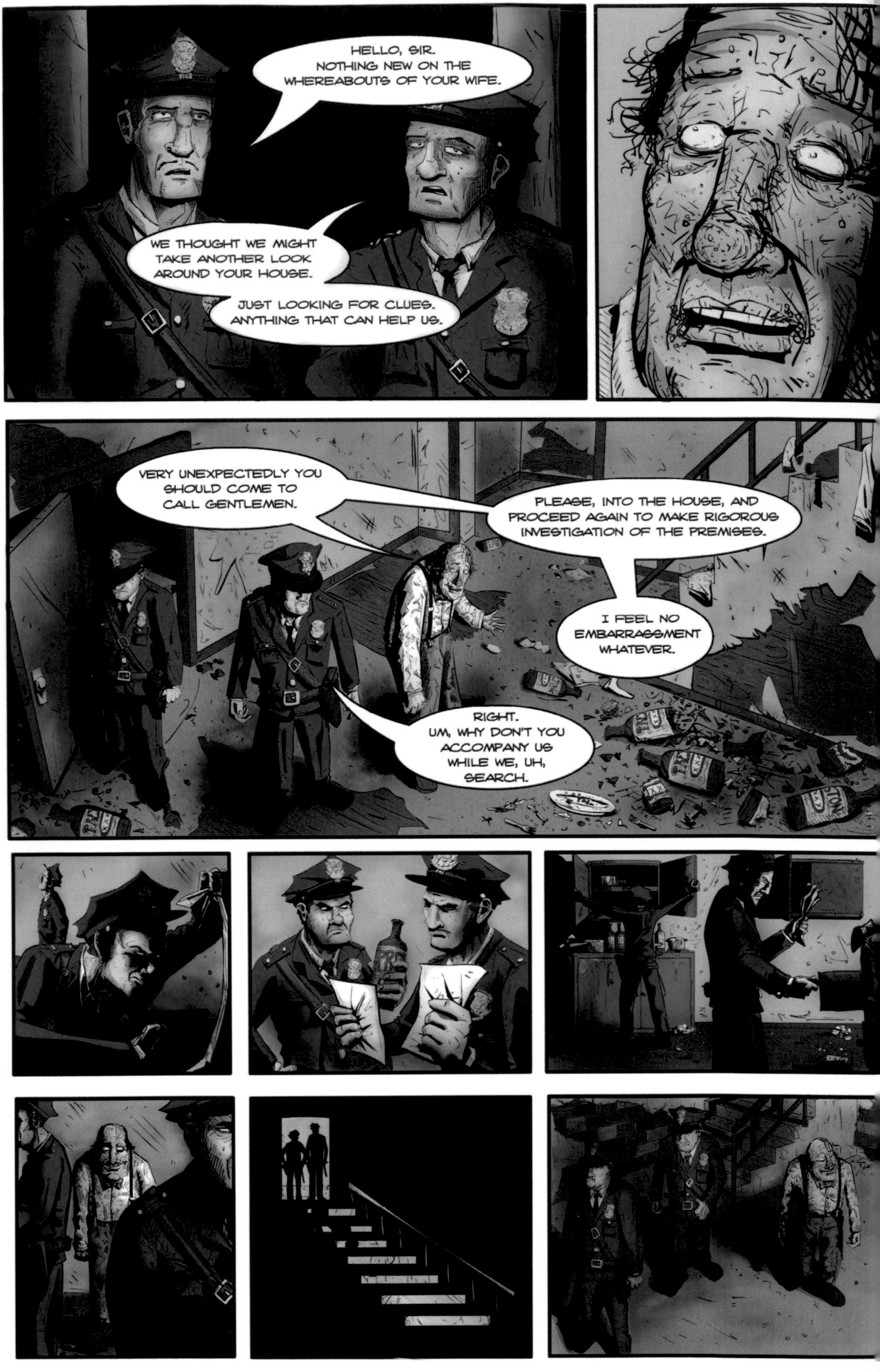
HELLO, SIR.
NOTHING NEW ON THE WHEREABOUTS OF YOUR WIFE.
WE THOUGHT WE MIGHT TAKE ANOTHER LOOK AROUND YOUR HOUSE.
JUST LOOKING FOR CLUES. ANYTHING THAT CAN HELP US.
VERY UNEXPECTEDLY YOU SHOULD COME TO CALL GENTLEMEN.
PLEASE, INTO THE HOUSE, AND PROCEED AGAIN TO MAKE RIGOROUS INVESTIGATION OF THE PREMISES.
I FEEL NO EMBARRASSMENT WHATEVER.
RIGHT.
UM, WHY DON'T YOU ACCOMPANY US WHILE WE, UH, SEARCH.

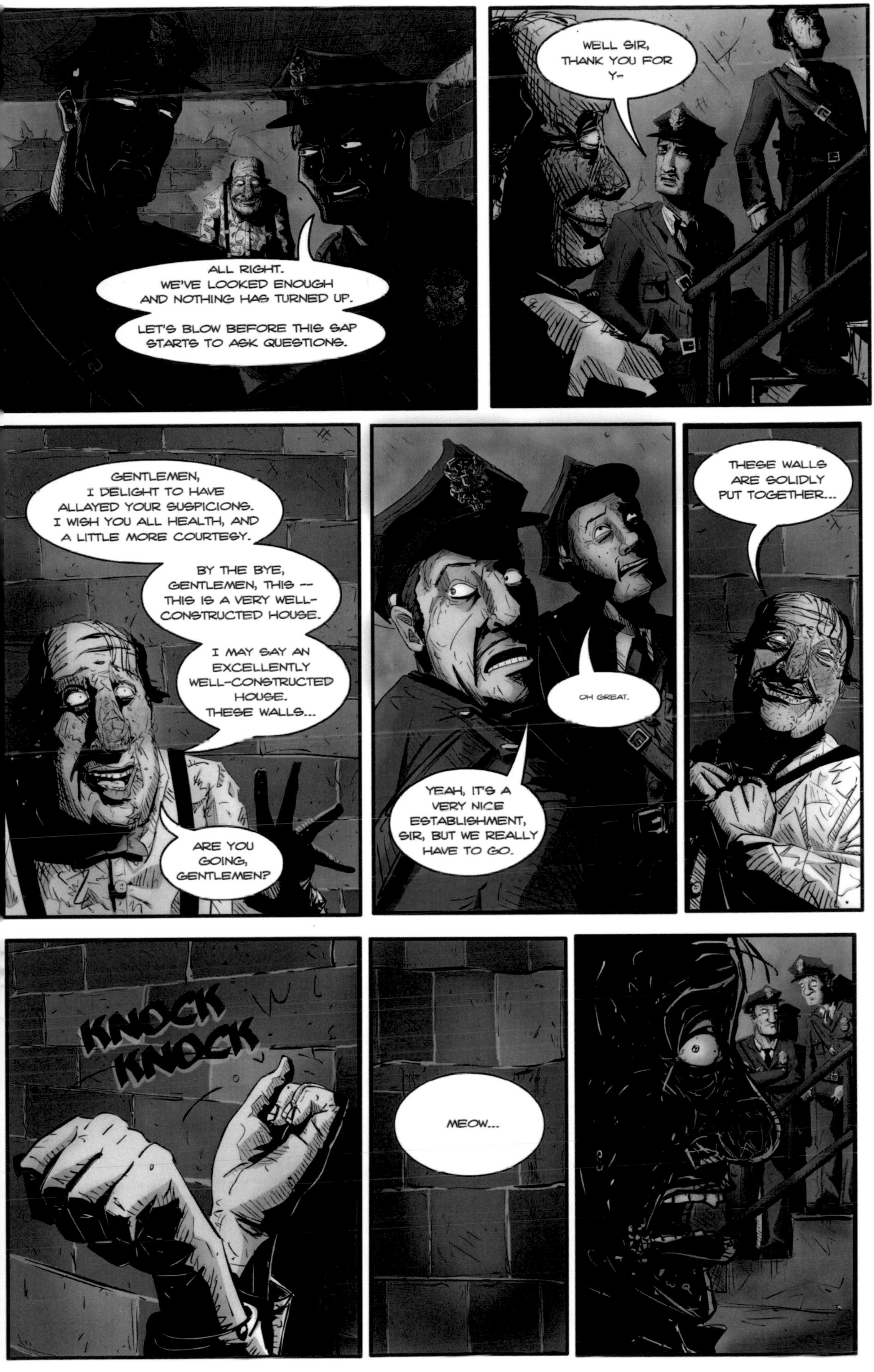
ALL RIGHT. WE'VE LOOKED ENOUGH AND NOTHING HAS TURNED UP.
LET'S BLOW BEFORE THIS SAP STARTS TO ASK QUESTIONS.
WELL SIR, THANK YOU FOR Y-
GENTLEMEN, I DELIGHT TO HAVE ALLAYED YOUR SUSPICIONS. I WISH YOU ALL HEALTH, AND A LITTLE MORE COURTESY.
BY THE BYE, GENTLEMEN, THIS -- THIS IS A VERY WELL-CONSTRUCTED HOUSE.
I MAY SAY AN EXCELLENTLY WELL-CONSTRUCTED HOUSE. THESE WALLS...
ARE YOU GOING, GENTLEMEN?
OH GREAT.
YEAH, IT'S A VERY NICE ESTABLISHMENT, SIR, BUT WE REALLY HAVE TO GO.
THESE WALLS ARE SOLIDLY PUT TOGETHER...
KNOCK KNOCK
MEOW...

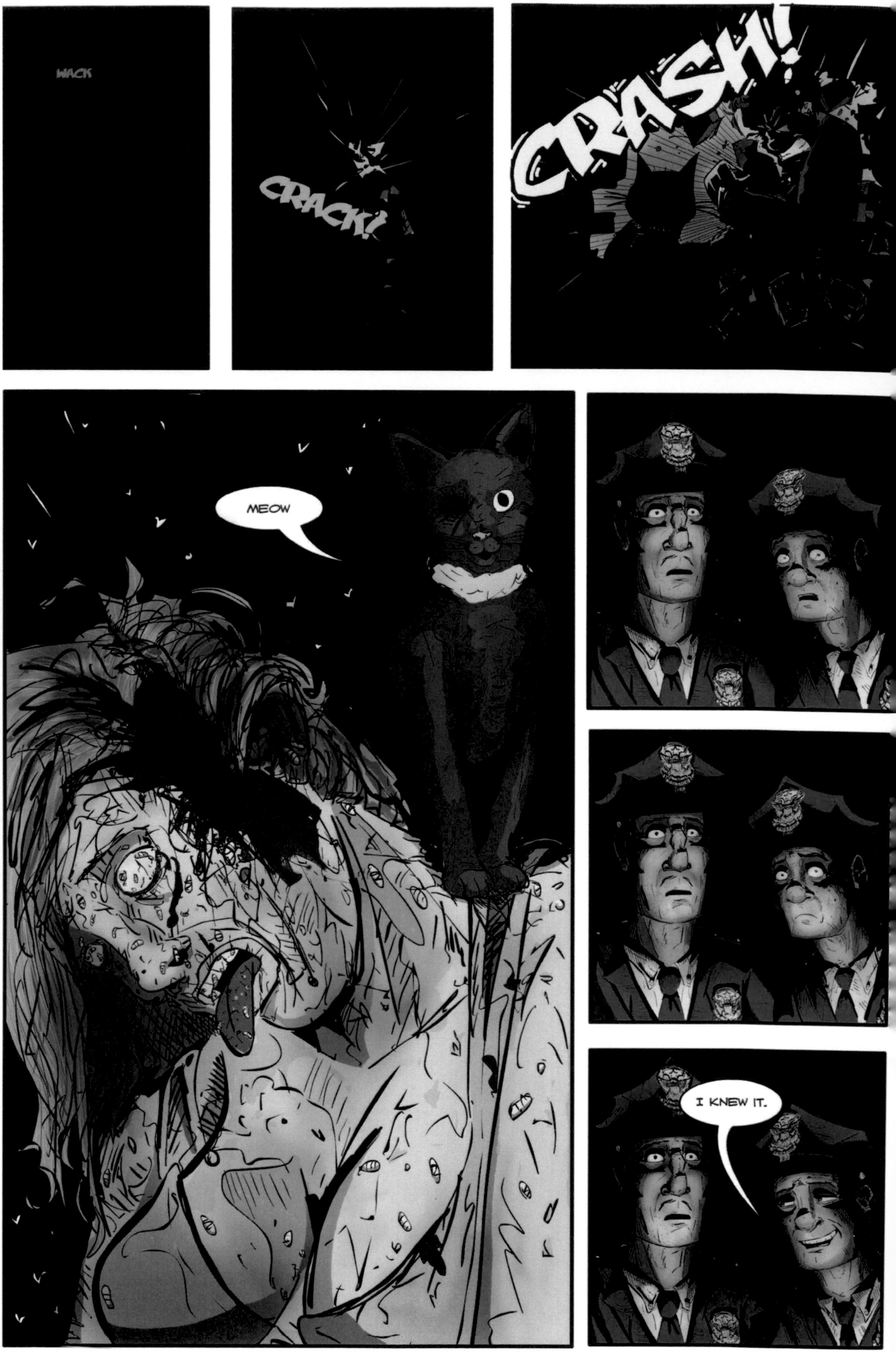
WACK
CRACK!
CRASH!
MEOW
I KNEW IT.

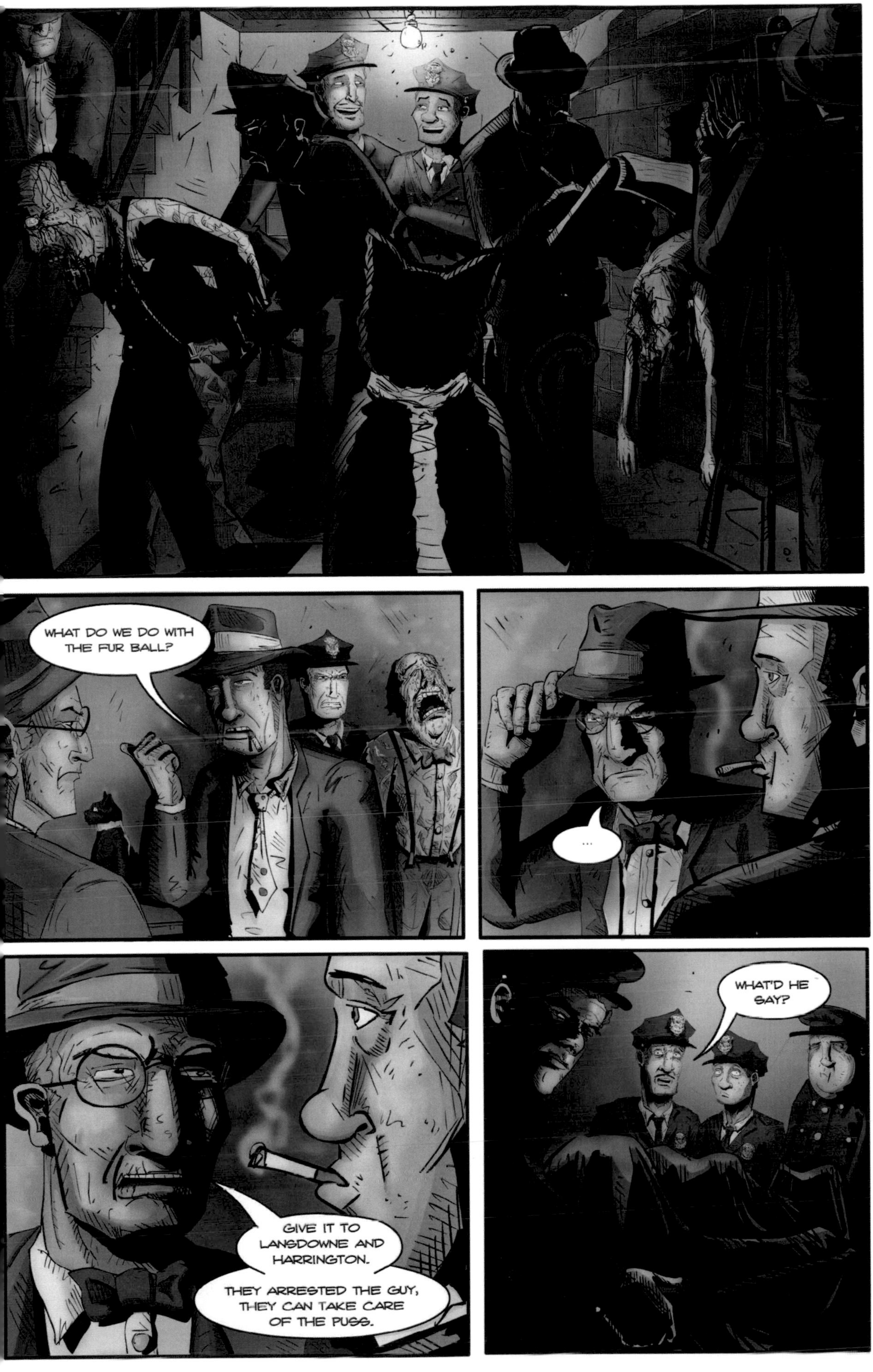
WHAT DO WE DO WITH THE FUR BALL?
...
GIVE IT TO LANSDOWNE AND HARRINGTON.
THEY ARRESTED THE GUY, THEY CAN TAKE CARE OF THE PUSS.
WHAT'D HE SAY?

I'M JUST TICKLED PINK WITH THIS CAT. HE'S JUST ACES!

WHAT ARE WE GOING TO NAME IT?

JUST CALL IT WHAT IT IS. 'CAT'.

HOW 'BOUT 'GUNPOWDER'?

THAT'S NO GOOD. YOU CAN'T NAME SOMETHING GUNPOWDER.

WHY NOT?

BECAUSE IT'S NOT A NAME!

WE CAN NAME IT WHATEVER WE WANT.

IT'S NOT LIKE IT'LL COME TO US WHEN WE CALL FOR IT.

IT WON'T? THEN WHAT'S THE POINT OF NAMING IT AT ALL?

I LIKE THE NAME GUNPOWDER.

I LIKE THE NAME "POUND."

DO YOU TAKE CATS TO THE POUND, OR IS THAT JUST DOGS?

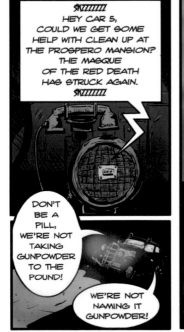

SKZZZZZ
HEY CAR 5, COULD WE GET SOME HELP WITH CLEAN UP AT THE PROSPERO MANSION? THE MASQUE OF THE RED DEATH HAS STRUCK AGAIN.
SKZZZZZ

DON'T BE A PILL, WE'RE NOT TAKING GUNPOWDER TO THE POUND!

WE'RE NOT NAMING IT GUNPOWDER!

WELL WHAT DO YOU SUGGEST?

HOW BOUT... IT'LL BE CALLED CHARLIE.

WHAT IF IT'S A GIRL?

WHAT IF IT IS?

GUNPOWDER CAN BE EITHER OR.

TO SHOOT A GUN. WHAT GUNPOWDER ISN'T IS A NAME.

YOU WILL NEVER STOP THE MASQUE OF THE RED DEATH!

BRRAAAMAAAAKKAT

GUNPOWDER IS A BETTER NAME THAN CHARLIE.

IT'S AT LEAST MANLIER.

BUT CHARLIE IS A MAN'S NAME.

BOOM BOOM

WE CAN COME UP WITH ANYTHING WE WANT AND YOU THINK UP CHARLIE?

GIVE ME A BREAK.

BOOM

D'OOM

BOOM

AW, BUTTON UP!

FINE. IF THAT'S THE CASE, HOW ABOUT...

SALTSHAKER.

THAT MAKES AS MUCH SENSE.

I KIND OF LIKE IT.

CLICK

OH YEAH? WAIT, NO!

WE'RE NOT NAMING IT SALTSHAKER OR GUNPOWDER OR ANYTHING ELSE!

WE'RE TAKING IT TO THE POUND!

IN A PIG'S EYE! WE'RE KEEPING IT!

AHHH!

SKIIII CAR 5, DOMESTIC DISTURBANCE AT 15 QUINT AVE. SKIIII

HEY RELAX. CATS BASICALLY TAKE CARE OF THEMSELVES.

ALL WE GOT TO DO IS FEED IT.

WHAT DO CATS EVEN EAT? TUNA?

HELLO, SIR. A NEIGHBOR REPORTED A SCREAM FROM THE PREMISES AND--

I BID THE GENTLEMEN WELCOME.

THE SHRIEK, WAS MY OWN IN A DREAM.

THE OLD MAN IS ABSENT IN THE COUNTRY.

I BID YOU TO SEARCH -- SEARCH WELL!

OH BOY.

WE CAN'T BUY TUNA EVERY DAY FOR A CAT.

CAN THEY SKIP A FEW DAYS?

MAYBE. NOT SURE.

HEY, NO SWEAT. I'LL FEED IT AND YOU TAKE CARE OF THE LITTER.

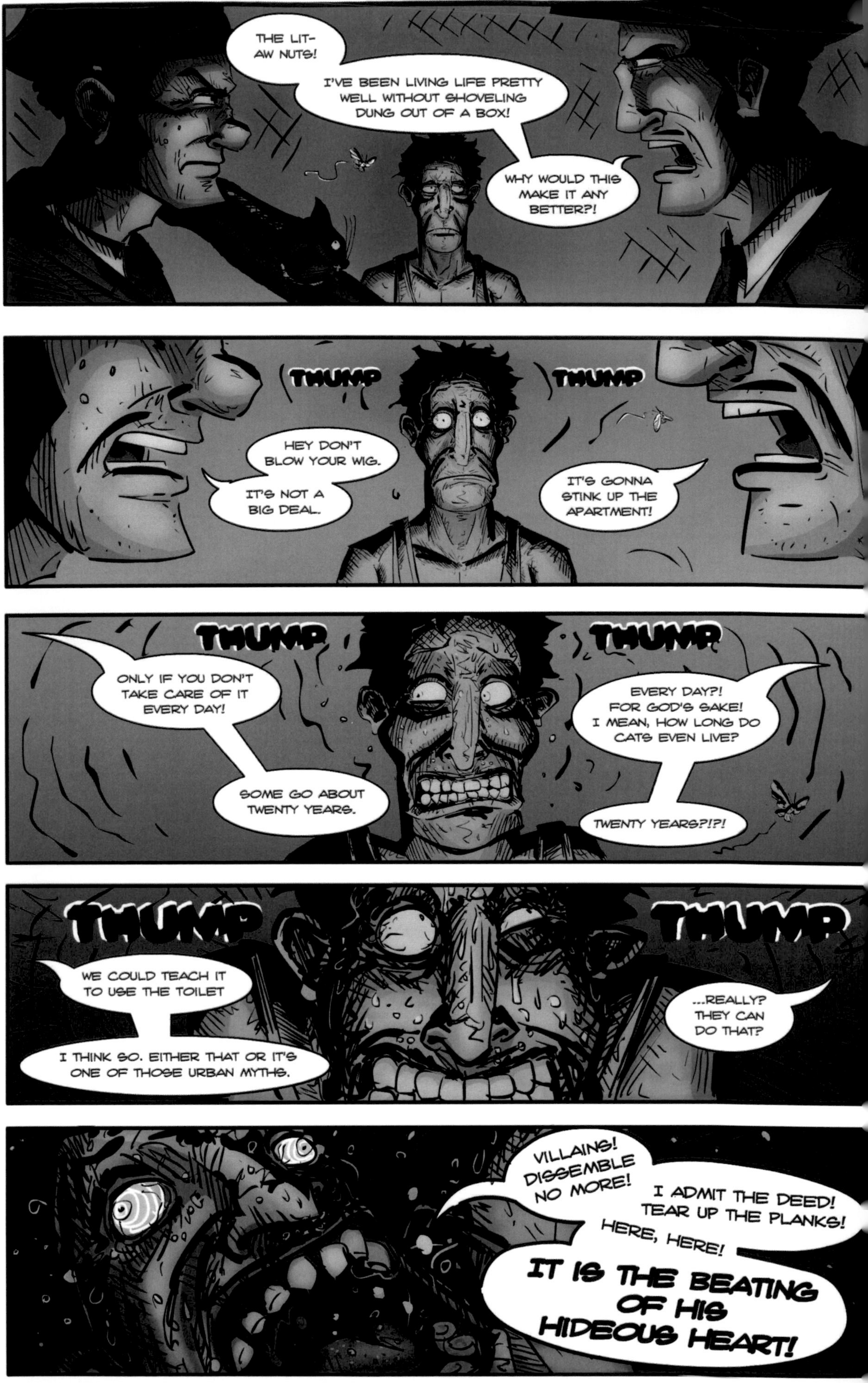
THE LIT-AW NUTS!
I'VE BEEN LIVING LIFE PRETTY WELL WITHOUT SHOVELING DUNG OUT OF A BOX!
WHY WOULD THIS MAKE IT ANY BETTER?!
THUMP
THUMP
HEY DON'T BLOW YOUR WIG.
IT'S NOT A BIG DEAL.
IT'S GONNA STINK UP THE APARTMENT!
THUMP
THUMP
ONLY IF YOU DON'T TAKE CARE OF IT EVERY DAY!
EVERY DAY?! FOR GOD'S SAKE! I MEAN, HOW LONG DO CATS EVEN LIVE?
SOME GO ABOUT TWENTY YEARS.
TWENTY YEARS?!?!
THUMP
THUMP
WE COULD TEACH IT TO USE THE TOILET
...REALLY? THEY CAN DO THAT?
I THINK SO. EITHER THAT OR IT'S ONE OF THOSE URBAN MYTHS.
VILLAINS! DISSEMBLE NO MORE!
I ADMIT THE DEED! TEAR UP THE PLANKS!
HERE, HERE!
IT IS THE BEATING OF HIS HIDEOUS HEART!

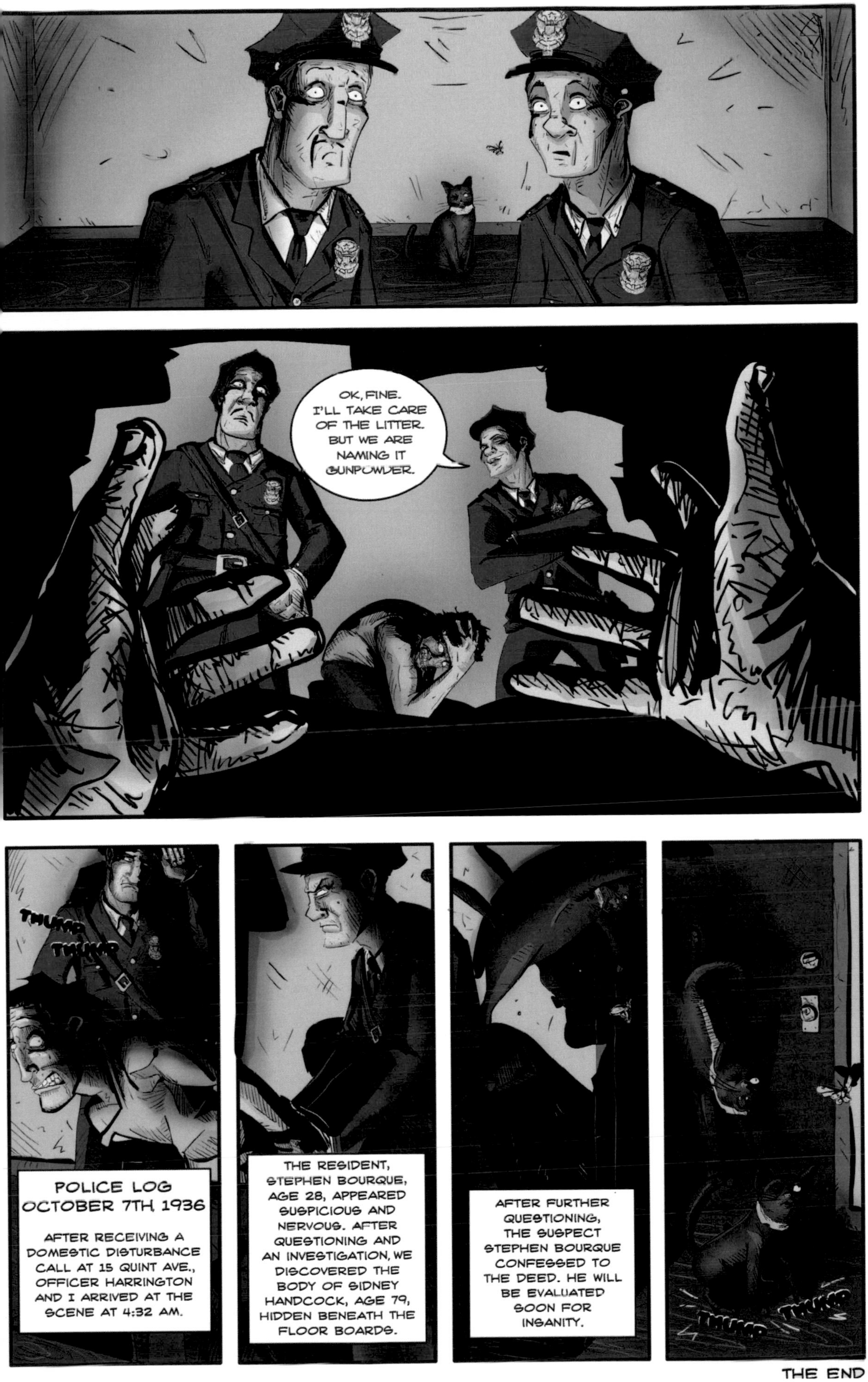
OK, FINE. I'LL TAKE CARE OF THE LITTER. BUT WE ARE NAMING IT GUNPOWDER.
THUMP
THUMP
POLICE LOG
OCTOBER 7TH, 1936
AFTER RECEIVING A DOMESTIC DISTURBANCE CALL AT 15 QUINT AVE., OFFICER HARRINGTON AND I ARRIVED AT THE SCENE AT 4:32 AM.
THE RESIDENT, STEPHEN BOURQUE, AGE 28, APPEARED SUSPICIOUS AND NERVOUS. AFTER QUESTIONING AND AN INVESTIGATION, WE DISCOVERED THE BODY OF SIDNEY HANDCOCK, AGE 79, HIDDEN BENEATH THE FLOOR BOARDS.
AFTER FURTHER QUESTIONING, THE SUSPECT STEPHEN BOURQUE CONFESSED TO THE DEED. HE WILL BE EVALUATED SOON FOR INSANITY.
THUMP
THUMP

THE END

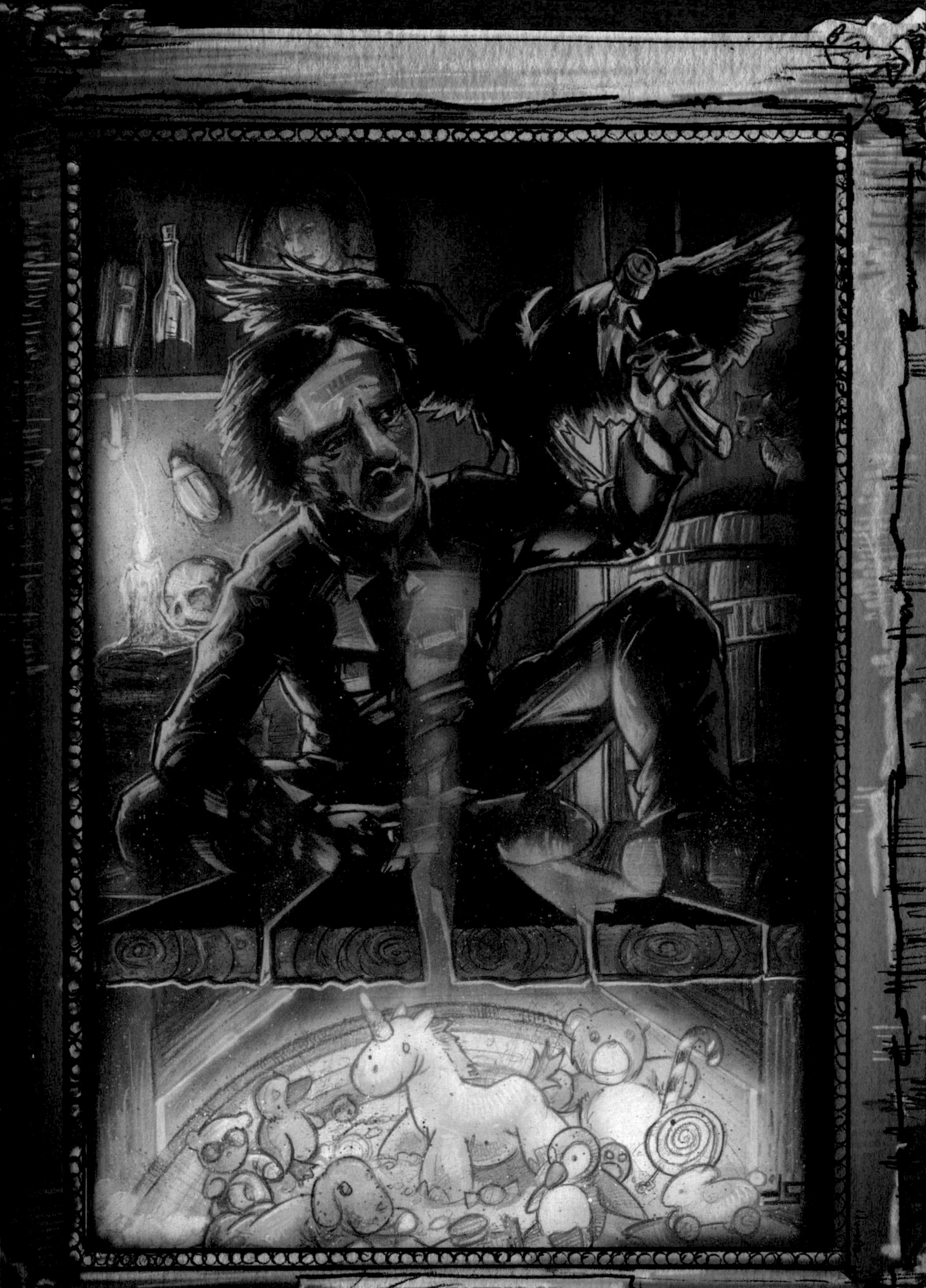

THE BEATING OF
THE HIDEOUS CUTENESS

THE TABLE WAS SUPERBLY SET OUT. IT WAS LOADED WITH PLATE, AND MORE THAN LOADED WITH DELICACIES. THE PROFUSION WAS ABSOLUTELY BARBARIC.

from "THE SYSTEM OF DOCTOR TARR AND PROFESSOR FETHER"

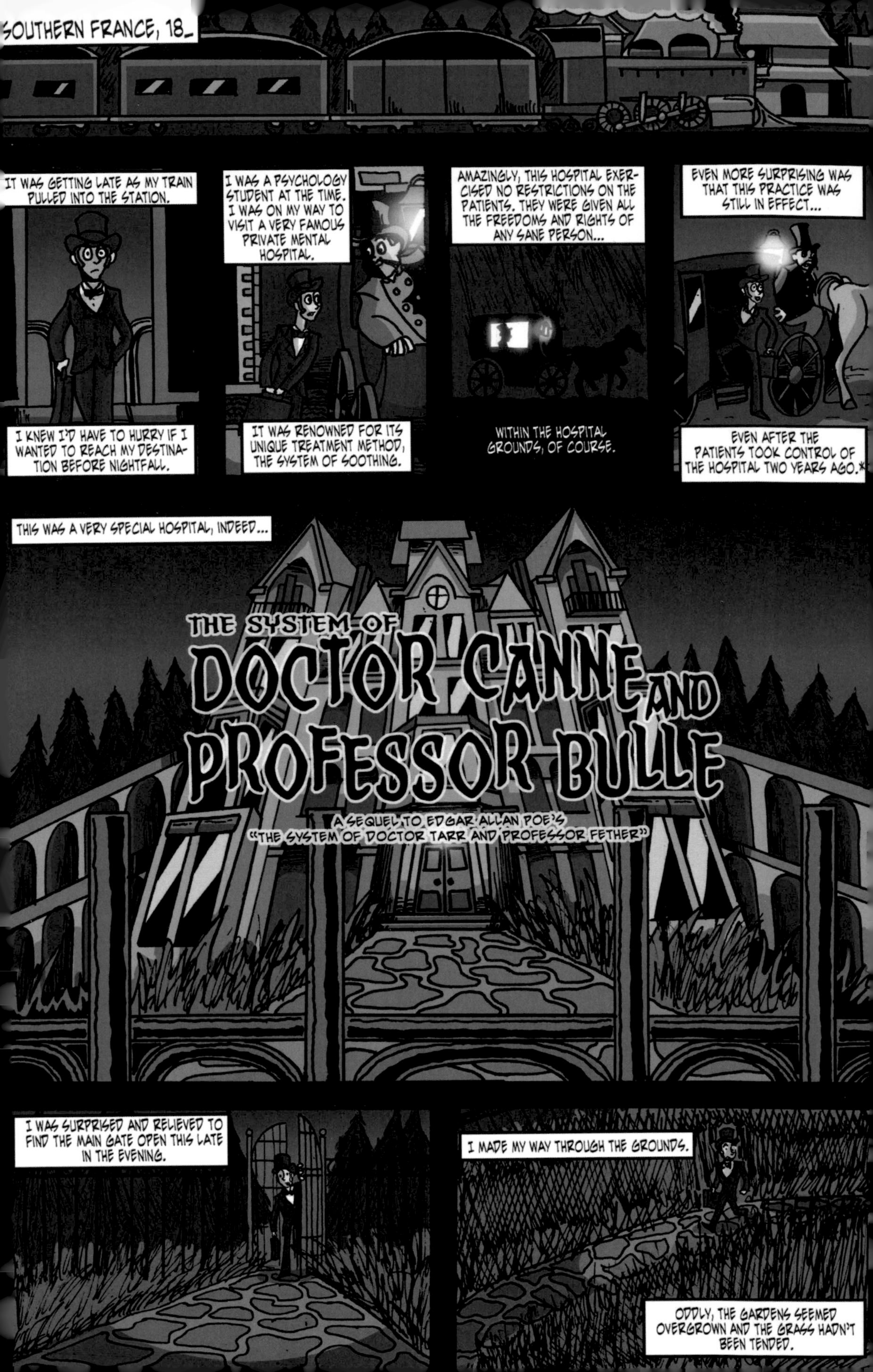
SOUTHERN FRANCE, 18_
IT WAS GETTING LATE AS MY TRAIN PULLED INTO THE STATION.
I KNEW I'D HAVE TO HURRY IF I WANTED TO REACH MY DESTINATION BEFORE NIGHTFALL.
I WAS A PSYCHOLOGY STUDENT AT THE TIME. I WAS ON MY WAY TO VISIT A VERY FAMOUS PRIVATE MENTAL HOSPITAL.
IT WAS RENOWNED FOR ITS UNIQUE TREATMENT METHOD, THE SYSTEM OF SOOTHING.
AMAZINGLY, THIS HOSPITAL EXERCISED NO RESTRICTIONS ON THE PATIENTS. THEY WERE GIVEN ALL THE FREEDOMS AND RIGHTS OF ANY SANE PERSON...
WITHIN THE HOSPITAL GROUNDS, OF COURSE.
EVEN MORE SURPRISING WAS THAT THIS PRACTICE WAS STILL IN EFFECT...
EVEN AFTER THE PATIENTS TOOK CONTROL OF THE HOSPITAL TWO YEARS AGO.*
THIS WAS A VERY SPECIAL HOSPITAL, INDEED...
THE SYSTEM OF
DOCTOR CANNE AND
PROFESSOR BULLE
A SEQUEL TO EDGAR ALLAN POE'S
"THE SYSTEM OF DOCTOR TARR AND PROFESSOR FETHER"
I WAS SURPRISED AND RELIEVED TO FIND THE MAIN GATE OPEN THIS LATE IN THE EVENING.
I MADE MY WAY THROUGH THE GROUNDS.
ODDLY, THE GARDENS SEEMED OVERGROWN AND THE GRASS HADN'T BEEN TENDED.

I CAME TO THE OAK FRONT DOORS AND KNOCKED...

I'M SORRY, BUT VISITORS ARE NOT PERMITTED.

BUT, SIR, I AM A STUDENT. I'VE TRAVELED FAR TO VISIT YOUR HOSPITAL.

... DO YOU HAVE FAMILY COMMITTED HERE?

NO, SIR. ALL MY FAMILY IS IN ENGLAND...

AH, WELL IN THAT CASE, PLEASE COME IN.

TEA?

HE INTRODUCED HIMSELF AS DR. EDWARDS, THOUGH HE NEEDN'T HAVE. I KNEW HIM ALL TOO WELL FROM MY STUDIES. HAILING FROM MY OWN NATIVE ENGLAND, HE WAS A MOST ACCOMPLISHED PSYCHOLOGIST. IT WAS WIDELY KNOWN THAT HE HAD BEEN ACTING AS HEAD OF THIS HOSPITAL FOR SEVERAL YEARS.

SHORTLY...

I'M SORRY TO HEAR YOUR HEART SO SET UPON SEEING OUR SYSTEM OF SOOTHING. WE HAVE NOT USED THAT PRACTICE FOR THE BETTER PART OF A YEAR.

PLEASE FORGIVE MY DISAPPOINTMENT. I WAS LOOKING FORWARD TO SEEING IT IN ACTION.

AS YOU MAY HAVE HEARD, THE SYSTEM OF SOOTHING CAUSED MANY PROBLEMS.

YES, THE PATIENT MUTINY. HOW HORRIBLE FOR YOU ALL.

IT WAS. WE WERE LOCKED IN OUR CELLS, TARRED AND FEATHERED, AND TREATED LIKE ANIMALS. MY STAFF HASN'T BEEN THE SAME...

NEITHER HAVE I, TO BE HONEST.

THERE WERE, NATURALLY, MORE ESCAPE ATTEMPTS. I REALIZED THAT IT WAS MY STAFF THAT REALLY NEEDED HELP. SO I DEVELOPED A NEW SYSTEM.

IF I MAY ASK, SIR, WHAT IS THIS NEW SYSTEM?

AH, NOW THAT IS AN EXPLANATION YOU COULD ONLY TRULY APPRECIATE AFTER DINNER.

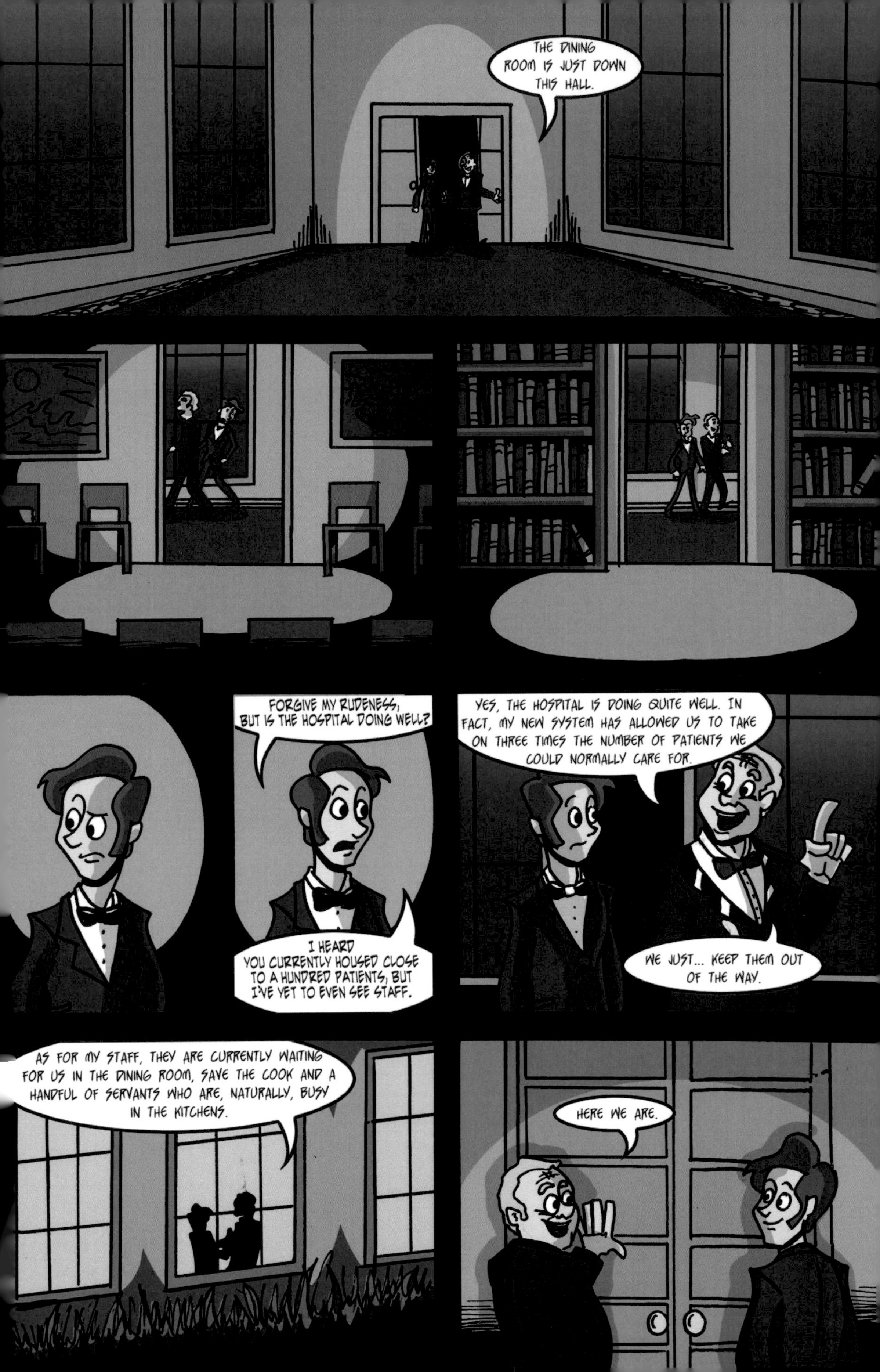
THE DINING ROOM IS JUST DOWN THIS HALL.
FORGIVE MY RUDENESS, BUT IS THE HOSPITAL DOING WELL?
I HEARD YOU CURRENTLY HOUSED CLOSE TO A HUNDRED PATIENTS, BUT I'VE YET TO EVEN SEE STAFF.
YES, THE HOSPITAL IS DOING QUITE WELL. IN FACT, MY NEW SYSTEM HAS ALLOWED US TO TAKE ON THREE TIMES THE NUMBER OF PATIENTS WE COULD NORMALLY CARE FOR.
WE JUST... KEEP THEM OUT OF THE WAY.
AS FOR MY STAFF, THEY ARE CURRENTLY WAITING FOR US IN THE DINING ROOM, SAVE THE COOK AND A HANDFUL OF SERVANTS WHO ARE, NATURALLY, BUSY IN THE KITCHENS.
HERE WE ARE.

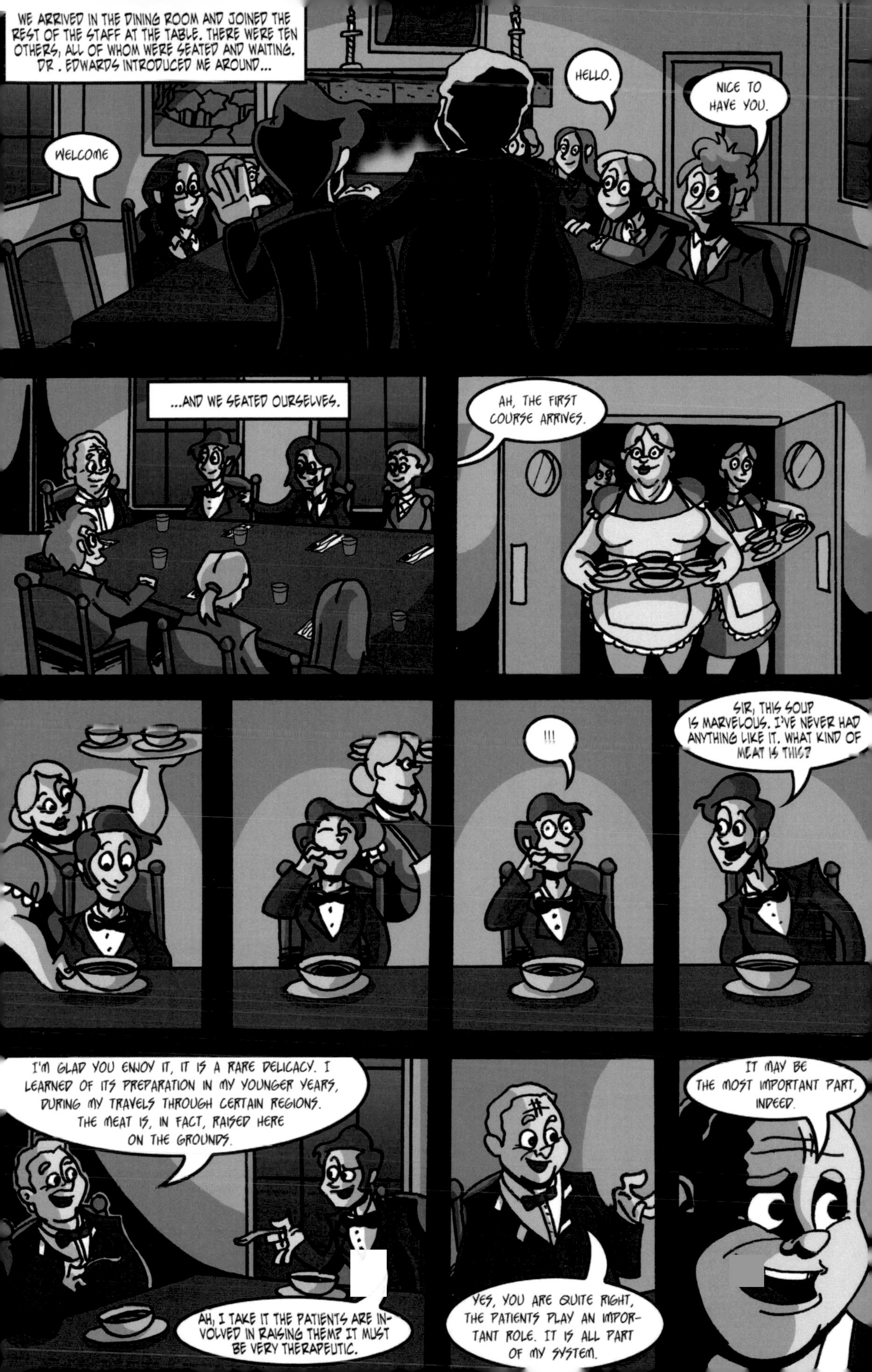
WE ARRIVED IN THE DINING ROOM AND JOINED THE REST OF THE STAFF AT THE TABLE. THERE WERE TEN OTHERS, ALL OF WHOM WERE SEATED AND WAITING. DR. EDWARDS INTRODUCED ME AROUND...
HELLO.
NICE TO HAVE YOU.
WELCOME
...AND WE SEATED OURSELVES.
AH, THE FIRST COURSE ARRIVES.
!!!
SIR, THIS SOUP IS MARVELOUS. I'VE NEVER HAD ANYTHING LIKE IT. WHAT KIND OF MEAT IS THIS?
I'M GLAD YOU ENJOY IT, IT IS A RARE DELICACY. I LEARNED OF ITS PREPARATION IN MY YOUNGER YEARS, DURING MY TRAVELS THROUGH CERTAIN REGIONS. THE MEAT IS, IN FACT, RAISED HERE ON THE GROUNDS.
AH, I TAKE IT THE PATIENTS ARE INVOLVED IN RAISING THEM? IT MUST BE VERY THERAPEUTIC.
YES, YOU ARE QUITE RIGHT, THE PATIENTS PLAY AN IMPORTANT ROLE. IT IS ALL PART OF MY SYSTEM.
IT MAY BE THE MOST IMPORTANT PART, INDEED.

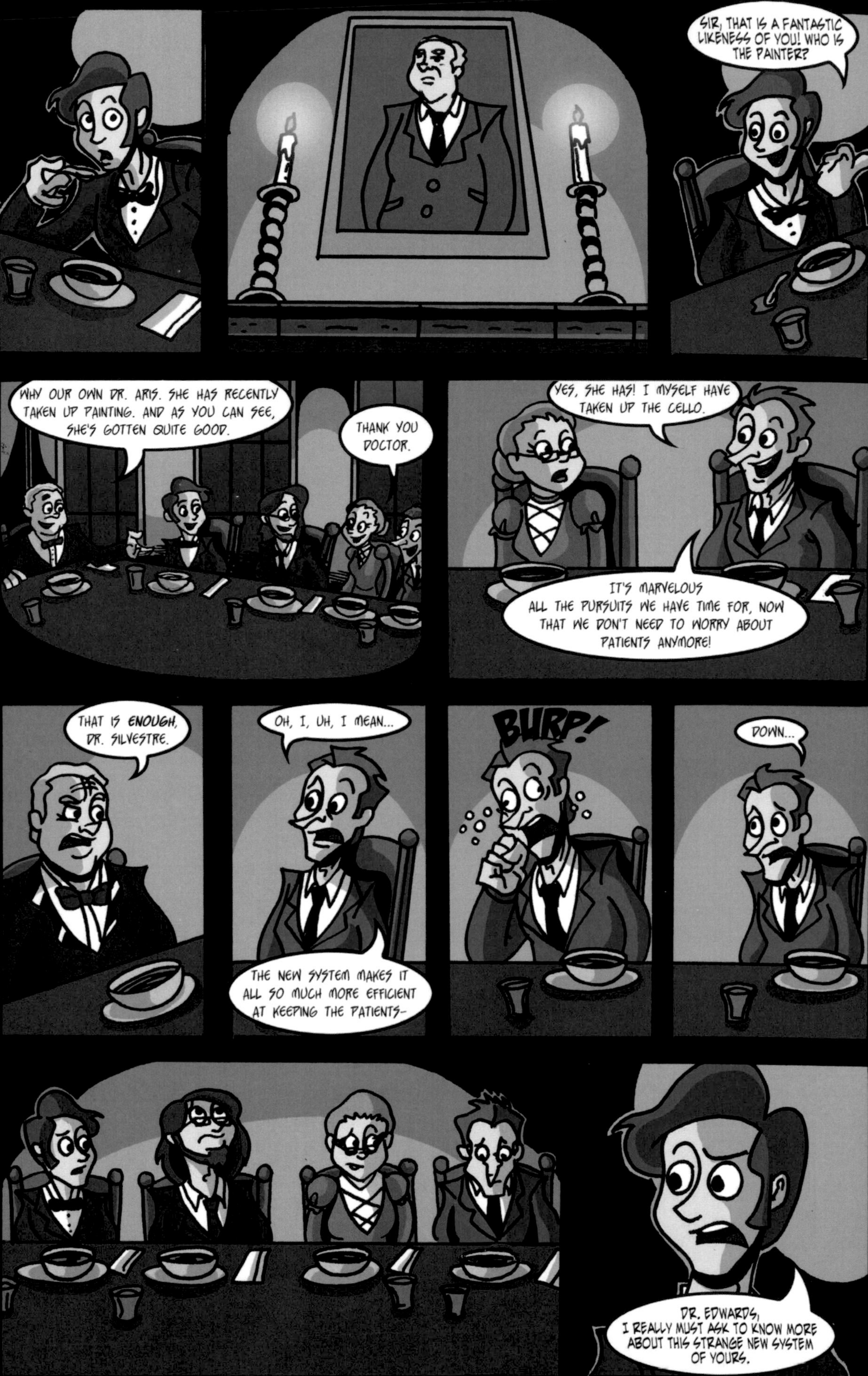
SIR, THAT IS A FANTASTIC LIKENESS OF YOU! WHO IS THE PAINTER?
WHY OUR OWN DR. ARIS. SHE HAS RECENTLY TAKEN UP PAINTING. AND AS YOU CAN SEE, SHE'S GOTTEN QUITE GOOD.
THANK YOU DOCTOR.
YES, SHE HAS! I MYSELF HAVE TAKEN UP THE CELLO.
IT'S MARVELOUS ALL THE PURSUITS WE HAVE TIME FOR, NOW THAT WE DON'T NEED TO WORRY ABOUT PATIENTS ANYMORE!
THAT IS ENOUGH, DR. SILVESTRE.
OH, I, UH, I MEAN...
THE NEW SYSTEM MAKES IT ALL SO MUCH MORE EFFICIENT AT KEEPING THE PATIENTS-
BURP!
DOWN...
DR. EDWARDS, I REALLY MUST ASK TO KNOW MORE ABOUT THIS STRANGE NEW SYSTEM OF YOURS.

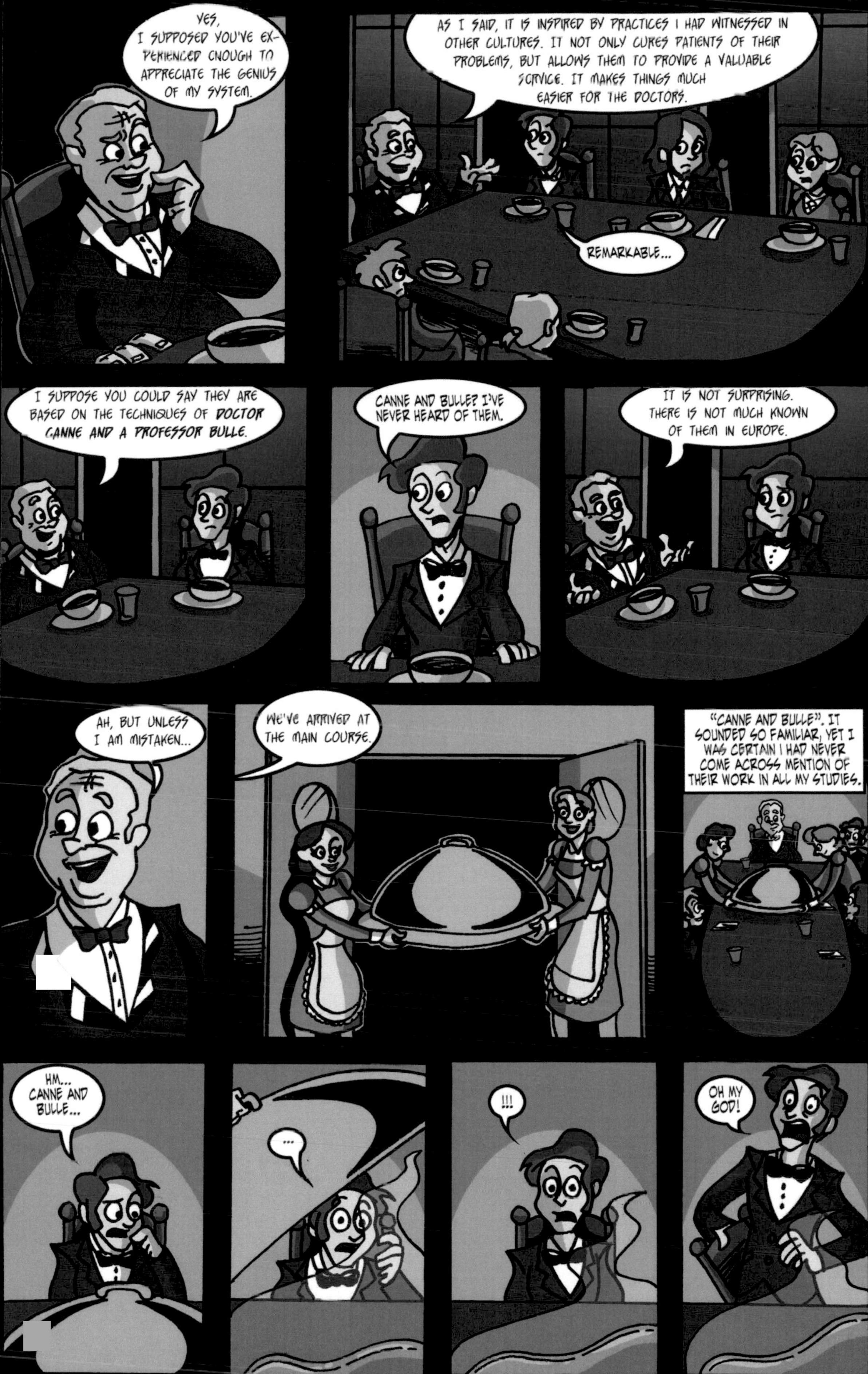
YES, I SUPPOSED YOU'VE EXPERIENCED ENOUGH TO APPRECIATE THE GENIUS OF MY SYSTEM.
AS I SAID, IT IS INSPIRED BY PRACTICES I HAD WITNESSED IN OTHER CULTURES. IT NOT ONLY CURES PATIENTS OF THEIR PROBLEMS, BUT ALLOWS THEM TO PROVIDE A VALUABLE SERVICE. IT MAKES THINGS MUCH EASIER FOR THE DOCTORS.
REMARKABLE...
I SUPPOSE YOU COULD SAY THEY ARE BASED ON THE TECHNIQUES OF DOCTOR CANNE AND A PROFESSOR BULLE.
CANNE AND BULLE? I'VE NEVER HEARD OF THEM.
IT IS NOT SURPRISING. THERE IS NOT MUCH KNOWN OF THEM IN EUROPE.
AH, BUT UNLESS I AM MISTAKEN...
WE'VE ARRIVED AT THE MAIN COURSE.
"CANNE AND BULLE". IT SOUNDED SO FAMILIAR, YET I WAS CERTAIN I HAD NEVER COME ACROSS MENTION OF THEIR WORK IN ALL MY STUDIES.
HM... CANNE AND BULLE...
...
!!!
OH MY GOD!

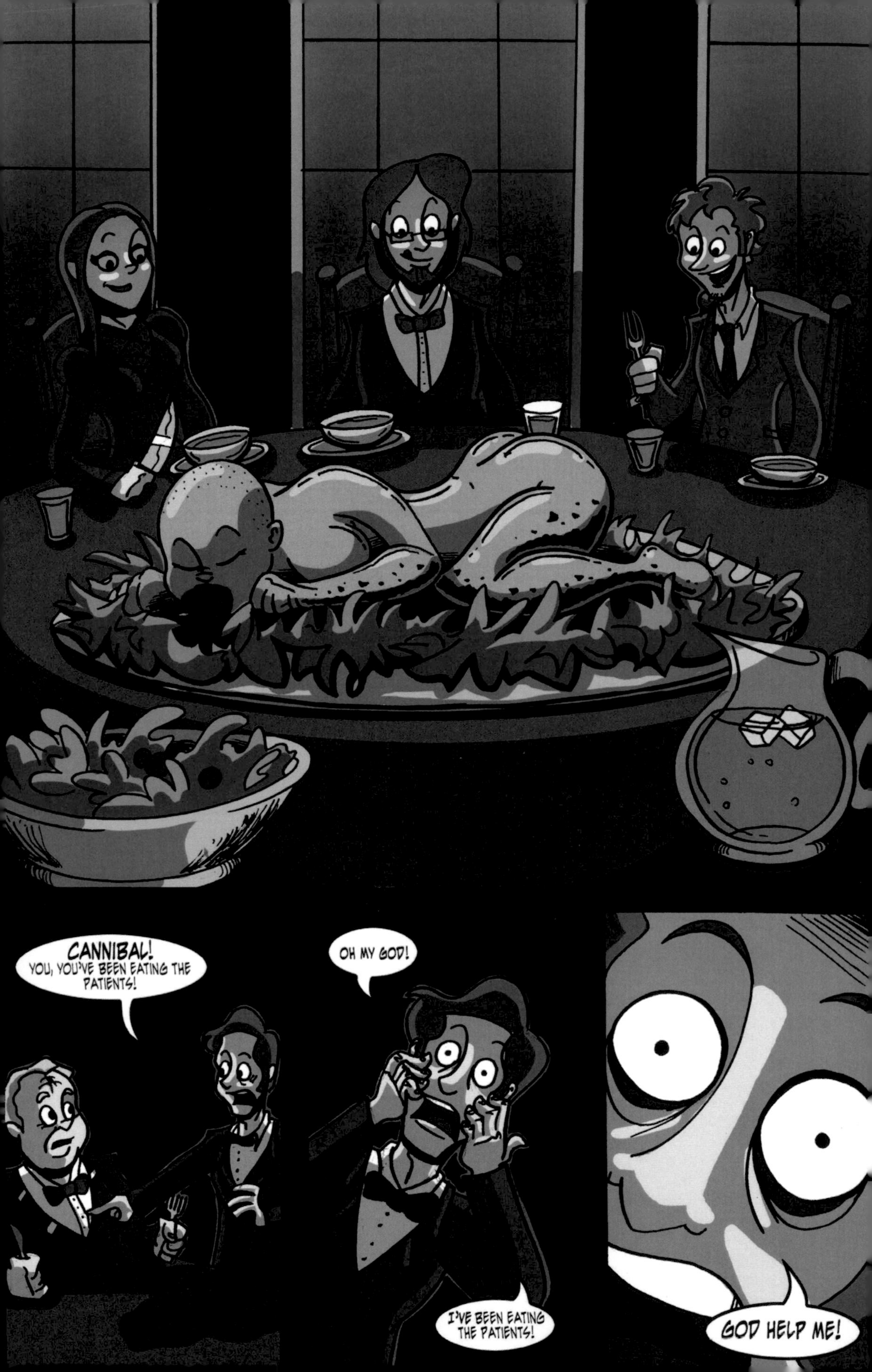
CANNIBAL!
YOU, YOU'VE BEEN EATING THE PATIENTS!
OH MY GOD!
I'VE BEEN EATING THE PATIENTS!
GOD HELP ME!

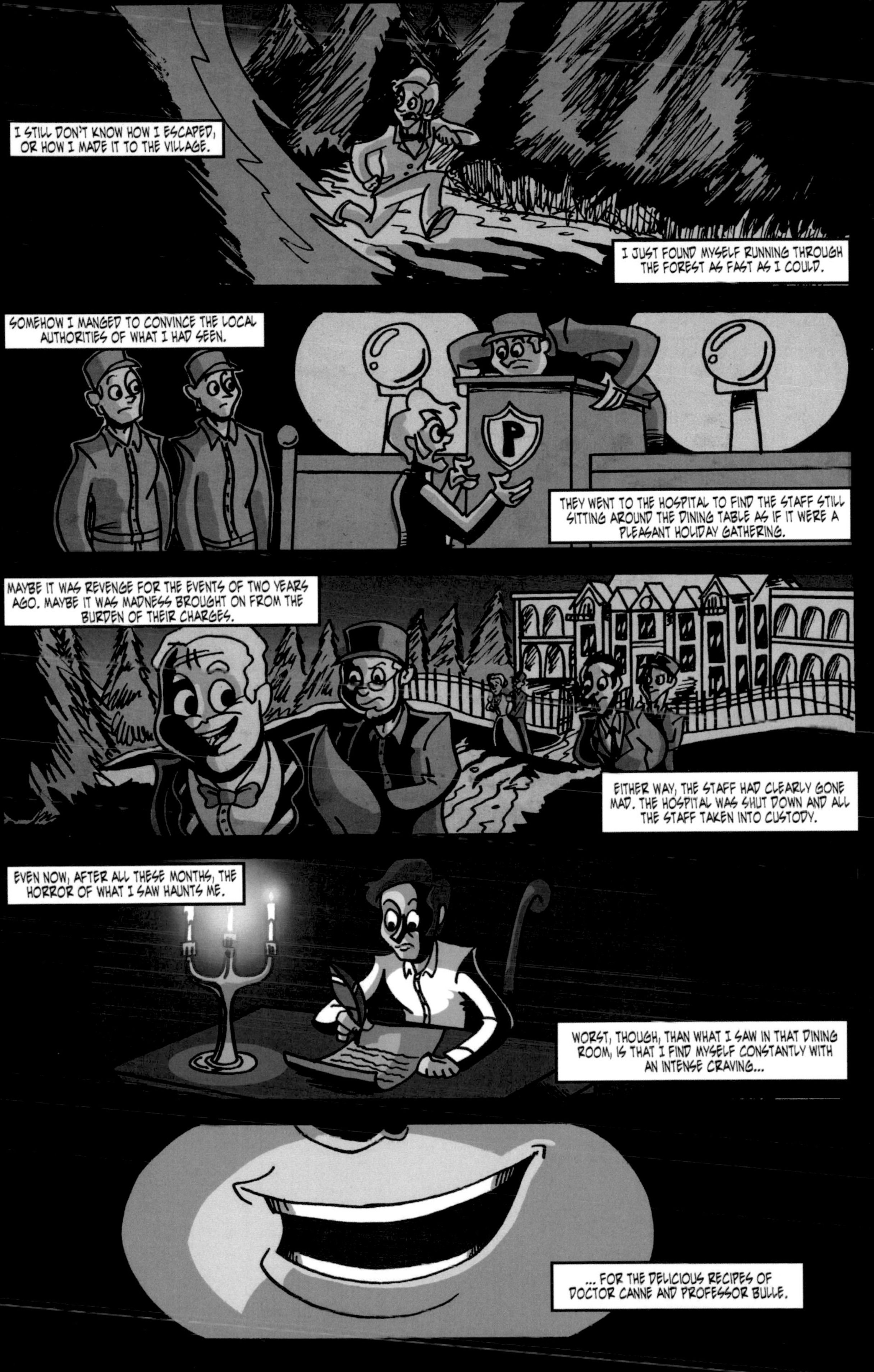
I STILL DON'T KNOW HOW I ESCAPED, OR HOW I MADE IT TO THE VILLAGE.
I JUST FOUND MYSELF RUNNING THROUGH THE FOREST AS FAST AS I COULD.
SOMEHOW I MANGED TO CONVINCE THE LOCAL AUTHORITIES OF WHAT I HAD SEEN.
P
THEY WENT TO THE HOSPITAL TO FIND THE STAFF STILL SITTING AROUND THE DINING TABLE AS IF IT WERE A PLEASANT HOLIDAY GATHERING.
MAYBE IT WAS REVENGE FOR THE EVENTS OF TWO YEARS AGO. MAYBE IT WAS MADNESS BROUGHT ON FROM THE BURDEN OF THEIR CHARGES.
EITHER WAY, THE STAFF HAD CLEARLY GONE MAD. THE HOSPITAL WAS SHUT DOWN AND ALL THE STAFF TAKEN INTO CUSTODY.
EVEN NOW, AFTER ALL THESE MONTHS, THE HORROR OF WHAT I SAW HAUNTS ME.
WORST, THOUGH, THAN WHAT I SAW IN THAT DINING ROOM, IS THAT I FIND MYSELF CONSTANTLY WITH AN INTENSE CRAVING...
... FOR THE DELICIOUS RECIPES OF DOCTOR CANNE AND PROFESSOR BULLE.

POE FOLK

ENRICA JANG is editor-in-chief at Red Stylo Media and the writer and creator of the *AZTECA* comic series. She is also screenwriter of the award-winning short film, *Frienemies (2011)*. Read her blog at EnricaJang.com.

THE POE TWISTED ANTHOLOGY, Editor

JASON CIARAMELLA is a 2011 Eisner Award-nominated writer of *The Cape* one-shot, *Kodiak*, and *The Cape* mini-series, from IDW. He makes his home with his two sons in The City of Champions, Massachusetts.

ABSOLUTION, writer

ALEX CORMACK is an illustrator/animator from Boston MA. His work has been seen all over the world in different publications, websites, and at festivals receiving awards and critical acclaim. He graduated from the Art Institute of Boston where he received a BFA in animation. For more information check out AlexCormack.com.

THE TELL TALE CAT, writer and artist
ELDORADO, artist
ABSOLUTION, cover design and color

ANDRE FRATTINO is artist and author of two graphic novels: *Flagler's Few and the Reaper of St. George Street* and the sequel, *Victor's Revenge*, from ARF Studios. He is also ink, color and letter-man for *AZTECA*, a comic series from Red Stylo Media. Andre lives in Gainesville, Florida.

ABSOLUTION, assistant editor and letterer

BENJAMIN FRAZIER has been drawing since he could hold a pencil, and through his father and mother, the love of comics started early. In 2000, Ben scored his first comic script to illustrate and has been hooked ever since.

THE AFTER PARTY, artist

PHILLIP JACOBSON was born and raised in Dallas, Texas. He graduated in 2011 with a BFA in Sequential Art from the Savannah College of Art & Design. He plans to pursue his MFA at SCAD as well. Though predominantly a comic artist, Phillip also enjoys storyboarding, character design, and playing Pokemon.

DEAD MAN'S HAND, writer and artist

ANDREW JERZ has done editorial work for a number of publications mostly headquartered between Springfield MA and Buffalo NY, at equally spaced intervals along the I-90 corridor (once known as the Mohawk Trail and, at some points, the Erie Canal). He has lived in Boston City with his illustrious Common Sense Advisor, Susan, since the rare old times.

LENORE, artist
CAREFUL COFFINS FOR THE CONCERNED CATALEPTIC, artist
AMONSTRILLADO, artist

MARK MULLANEY is an artist from Boston, Massachussetts. See more of his work at themahk.blogspot.com.

ZOMBIE CRUISE, artist
THE AFTER PARTY, color and letters
THE SYSTEM OF DOCTOR CANNE AND PROFESSOR BULLE,
writer and artist

KYLE RICHEY is a freelance writer and author. He resides in Maple Shade NJ, and is currently at work on his own self-published series, *Accord*, a Cold-War era action/love story.

THE AFTER PARTY, writer

ENRIQUE "ZEKE" SAVORY, JR., is a comic veteran and international man of mystery. Zeke's credits include *The Rift* and *Totem* comic series.

ABSOLUTION, artist

DIRK STRANGELY is a multimedia artist and the creator of many independent comics, including *Graveyard Girl* . He lives with his family in Florida.

POE TWISTED CAT #1-3, artist
POE TWISTED RAVEN #1-3, artist

JASON STRUTZ is an illustrator and artist for the comic series *The Order of Dagonet*, written by Jeremy Whitley. He lives with his wife/editor in Carrboro, NC. See more of his work at StrutzIllustration.com

UNUSUAL SUSPECT, artist
WHAT TOOK YOU SO LONG?, artist
THE BEATING OF THE HIDEOUS CUTENESS, artist

MARTA TANRIKULU edits and writes technical, educational, marketing, and creative materials, including the occasional story. Trained as a scientist, she worked as a researcher and editor in the biotech industry before founding her company, TanMar Editorial.

ZOMBIE CRUISE, writer

SHEREZADA WINDHAM-KENT is a writer and filmmaker living and working in the San Francisco Bay Area. Her short film, *Everything I Needed to Know About Zombies I Learned From the Movies,* participated in film festivals in New York, Chicago, Milwaukee, and San Francisco in 2009.

ELDORADO, writer